Metric Engine

Reinventing Data Supply Chains for Business

A Monograph

By Kip M. Twitchell

Edited by

Randall H. Ness

Published 2015

Cover art: "downpour" by Lane Twitchell, oil, enamel and acrylic on cut melinex and polyester mesh mounted to oil and acrylic on panel. 48" x 48". 2012 © by Lane Twitchell, 2012.. Cover design by Lane Twitchell.

A Delta Summit Imprint

Printed by CreateSpace, an Amazon Company

ISBN: 978-0-9915701-3-3

Version 1.1.20150501

First Printing 2015

Metric Engine

Reinventing Data Supply Chains for Business

Kip Twitchell is also the author of *Balancing Act: A Practical Approach to Business Event Based Insights* (2011)

An attempt at simplicity,
inspired by my children

CONTENTS

PREFACE

The objective of this book is to identify and describe a *data supply chain* and propose the concept of a *metric engine* to dramatically empower it. The book explains the simple functions and principles which make the data supply chain necessary and outlines the importance of the ubiquitous (but now almost unnoticeable) business system processes known as posting. It then presents an alternative approach, informed by recent developments in textual analytics, of moving our quantitative reporting systems to metric engines, which behave much more like a search engine. After reading this book, if I am skillful enough in writing, the reader should see that consolidating data supply chains results in greater accuracy and better information, measurement, and performance at lower cost.

A data supply chain turns data into information and independent business events into actionable, measured understanding. Over the last 30 years data supply chains have proliferated, caused by the explosion of data and the need for more efficient actions. Yet often reports from different supply chains within the same business recommend different actions, if they provide enough clarity for any action at all. How is this possible given the supply chains share the vast majority of the input business events? This book explains why.

Data supply chain consolidation is inevitable, reversing trends in posting process proliferation. When it happens, it may create an entirely new industry, or at least significantly alter existing businesses, having an impact similar to that of search engines a generation ago. A better understanding of the simple principles of quantifying, posting, and aggregating data can enable consolidation. Those who invest in understanding these principles will be able to capture significant savings by eliminating duplicative supply chains, enabling more effective actions, and participating in the new world.

This work summarizes, simplifies, and builds upon material presented more exhaustively in my book, *Balancing Act: A Practical Approach to Business Event Based Insights*. I've written this new work for the strategist, to provide an overview of the principles which were elaborated with detailed examples for the practitioner in that earlier work. Paraphrasing the French mathematician and philosopher Blaise Pascal, I made the first book longer because I had not the time to make it shorter. Do not be misled by the brevity of this second work. Reinventing the data supply chain requires most of the steps in one form or another as described in my earlier book, but all the essential steps are included here in summary.

Although this book proposes taking the systems described in that work farther, this is not a theoretical work. This type of system is functioning today in many fundamental ways described in this book at more than one organization.

That book tells the story of the contributions of many people towards development of my understanding of this subject through decades of practical experience. I hope that this work makes that knowledge more approachable by focusing on the key concepts involved.

Chapter 1

QUANTIFICATION

The Basis of Business Measurement

Quantified metrics influence our lives every day. A very simple example of this is when we dress differently after checking the outside temperature. Temperature is a quantified metric.

There was a time, not that long ago, when the concepts of "hot" and "cold" did not equate to 110 and -20 degrees Fahrenheit. Temperatures were born when someone divided the responses of fluids to hot and cold into quanta—small consistent sections—and assigned each section a number.

This development was a continuation of a general trend of quantification that directed building efforts for significant portion of the modern world. Such thinking led others to realize that other things could be quantified: things then described only by qualitative terms, such as good or bad, effective or ineffective, responsive or unresponsive, fast or slow.

The process of quantifying continues to the present day. New metrics are introduced frequently: Quality of service ratings, standardized test scores, not to mention a host of financial measures, which are themselves quanta of various kinds. Much of business is nothing more than measuring the value—a type of quanta—of various behaviors, behaviors that create goods or provide services.

As we noted with temperature, measurement often changes behavior. Measuring and reporting over time typically lead to improvements in behavior. The expansion in what can be measured, tracked, and therefore managed has furthered the incredible prosperity of today. And there is no sign the trends are about to stop.

However, our prosperity would be increasing more quickly if it weren't being impeded by certain obstacles. Our ability to measure is hampered by the lack of access to "thermometers" of various kinds. And the accuracy of some existing types of "thermometers" could stand to be improved as well—significant errors may lead us to be "dressed" inappropriately at times.

The advent of computers accelerated quantification. The computer is especially good at tracking changes in quanta and at providing measurement at points in time. The first decades of business computer use included precisely these types of applications.

Computers are useful for more than just quantitative measurement. The last two decades have seen significant advances in *qualitative* computing—searching and finding words and text, as evidenced by the ubiquitous use of search engines. It is difficult to point to a similar type of innovation in *quantitative* computing: that which deals with numbers. For our most important financial metrics, we are using many of the same techniques, if not systems, first automated half a century ago.

Advances in our ability to measure, or quantitative analytics, are now often hampered by the inappropriate organization of the data—the quanta. Our ability to capture data continues to improve while our ability to organize it in meaningful ways for expanded quantitative analysis is not keeping up.

Consider the following simple and pervasive examples of well-known metrics in business today:

Revenues: Revenue, or what a specific customer pays for products or services, is captured by almost every business. Yet almost no business can say how much a specific customer has paid for their products or services over a period of time, be it their total time as a customer, or even just last year, last month, or last week. Most businesses lose track of the specific customer revenue very quickly simply by not retaining the data and thus cannot use it to measure the importance of a customer.

Risk and Forecast: Measuring and thus understanding what a customer has paid is not the same as predicting what they will do tomorrow. Businesses spend a significant amount of time trying to forecast, but wouldn't knowing customer revenue improve the predictions? And if we can't keep track of that, what other types of data that might improve our predictions do we drop, like specifics about products or services purchased, personal or family attributes, even information the customer willingly shared with us? We continually struggle to predict the future value and risk of a customer's business and then test how accurate our predictions were.

Profit: Revenue is one thing, but profit is quite another. One major difference is that profit takes into account the cost of the product or service. Costs are not typically accumulated by customers because we don't pay customers, we pay other people to produce the goods or services, like employees and vendors. Yet as in the case of customer-specific data, we often lose visibility to these activities and inputs, and things termed overhead. Without these measures, we are challenged to really measure and predict costs and then profitability.

Unit Costs: The difficulty in connecting costs to customers is a major impediment for managers of these service functions who are actually responsible for holding costs down. There are systems that do this today, but they do it in a very convoluted way. They are programmed by specialists often far removed from the real processes involved. The managers have little input into data drivers or allocation formulas, little ability to experiment with different types of formulas, data, and trends, and difficulty understanding the results produced from the existing systems. All this impedes true efficiencies in and across many, many business functions.

The weight of the inappropriately organized data shows up in the ever-expanding cost of producing today's defined metrics, let alone any additional costs for new metrics required to meet growing demands. Only by innovating can we hope to arrest the growing cost curve of measurement, which is well-known to chief financial and risk officers and others in many industries.

Understanding how data is organized today and what is required to provide measurement at any point in time is critical to finding a path to improve and expand quantitative computing and the resulting benefits to society.

Chapter 2

THE ASSEMBLY OF DATA

A Manufactured Goods Warehouse Analogy

Data is not a naturally occurring substance like water or rock. It is man-made from the outset. But, like naturally occurring raw materials, data becomes increasingly valuable as it is further refined and processed into manufactured goods, and as it is stored in various levels of finished forms for further assembly and use. So. let's think about the traditional approach to "manufacturing" data, and storing it in "warehouses."

We are all familiar with the creation of data; for example, we enter our name, credit card number, and desired flights when purchasing plane tickets. We know this data is stored somewhere and retrieved as we check in for our flight, but how else it is used and what other forms it may take is much less clear to most people.

These subsequent uses of data fascinate me.

Raw materials for manufacturing are in their most granular form and often in their most voluminous quantities, in their initial, raw state. Crude oil, raw silicon, gypsum, iron ore, each is a pile, with undifferentiated content and purpose before manufacturing begins.

Our initial creation of data is like these piles. Each airline reservation record is very similar to the one next to it. Yes, perhaps each record differs a bit more than the particles of iron ore differ in each nugget of ore, but the structure and contents of each record are very similar.

And just like mounds of ore, there are mounds of these kinds of records. Piles upon piles upon piles of them. Point of sale records from retail, cell phone call records in communications, ATM transactions in banking, and so on and so forth. All these exist in what might be termed "operational systems," systems where data is originally created. These systems contain the web pages and supporting databases we use to purchase the ticket and check-in for the flight.

Once produced, these piles of original, very specific, granular data can then begin their journeys toward reports of various kinds, representing manufactured end products in a retail store, if you will.

Portions of these piles of original data are shipped to one or more assembly lines, beginning initially with a subassembly rather than going directly to a final product.

These subassembly units are held in warehouses until additional manufacturing lines are ready to receive them. In the data world, these warehouses hold specific types of data. These warehouses are analytical systems, data repositories, data warehouse, or even simply reporting systems. The data they contain have yet to be manipulated in some further way for final presentation in reports of various sizes and shapes.

Our analogy isn't perfect. A particle of gypsum can only exist in one place at one time. But data doesn't have this constraint; copies of data are quite possible and in fact, we make them all the time.

These copies of data are not complete copies. For example, as the ticket data is run through the subassembly line, the credit card number may not be copied. This sensitive data is isolated and highly controlled. The potential impact to an organization for not doing so is significant. Some data is changed into other values, a translation from one computer "language" or encoding to another. For example, you might have entered "adult" when purchasing the ticket, but the copy might depict that as a "1" (and "2" for a child). The changed data most often is the same in substance to the original, but somewhat different in form, perhaps more refined, similar to the differences between crude oil and gasoline.

For the most part, the data becomes much less specific as it moves through manufacturing; for example, it may become less tied to a specific customer or event. Amounts are accumulated with other customer amounts. Typically, data and raw materials flow only in one direction. Even with recycling, materials are rarely turned back into the original form: the tree, the rock, the crude oil. The report manufacturing process also transforms and destroys the original materials. With data, once accumulated, an amount can't typically be "unaccumulated." If two numbers are added together on the assembly line and only the result is recorded or remembered, we can't be sure what the individual original inputs were.

The space in the quarries and mining sites is precious; space must be made for new materials being produced daily. The constant movement of raw materials is like deletion or loss of the original values in the operational systems. For example, a record of purchasing a ticket might be kept for a year, a record of checking in for the flight might only be kept a few weeks, and the record of the actual click of an on-line ad only for a day or less. Because the value of the data declines with age, the loss of original data occurs all along the manufacturing chain, in the subassembly process, the warehouses, all the way up to the retail stores. But the greatest reduction is from the original raw material piles.*

Rather than simply being deleted, a large amount of data is archived, which is a little bit like being turned into rock. Once the detailed data is archived, it could still be turned back into something more usable, but that would require much time and energy. Searching through archived data for the details requires pick and shovel-like tools.

The piece of the flight purchase data with the greatest impact, which is copied the most and travels the farthest and lasts the longest, is the amount paid for the ticket. The ripple effect of this amount, accumulated with the amounts other customers have paid, is very far-reaching. It ripples through and affects the earnings of the company per day, week, month, quarter and year; the revenue for the specific flight that day, month, and other periods; the total amount due from the credit card company, cash on hand, and other metrics.

This accumulation, transformation and mixing typically happens in the repositories—the sub-assembly lines and perhaps main assemble. The data is mixed in predictable patterns defined by the systems. The summarized fare paid by all the customers for a flight will end up next to the total cost of the flight, including fuel, personnel, and a portion of the aircraft costs. These two numbers will beg the question: did the company make money on that flight or not? Answering this question will cause another piece of data to be generated, and this will then likely be stored with the others in the warehouse,

* Data is different than raw materials, in that we can make copies of data rather than use up raw materials; but, if we then delete the original granular data after aggregating for a desired report the effect is the same.

not in the raw material piles. This value is not created in detail for each customer—only in aggregate for the entire flight.

This mixing in manufacturing might be thought of as creating new data, but for the most part, very few new things are entered in screens and stored directly in the warehouse; most inputs come from the piles, then through the subassemblies, and are stored in the warehouses.

These accumulated values are shipped to the final manufacturing assembly line, pulled there by someone looking for information of some kind. The data also becomes more and more specific to a single question, smaller in scope, less voluminous in quantity, and more narrowly defined, most often summarized as it approaches the store.

If you will, the data is ultimately carried from the store in a bag by hand—the hand of course, of someone needing some knowledge, looking perhaps for the profitability of a specific flight, an answer provided by precious pieces of data.

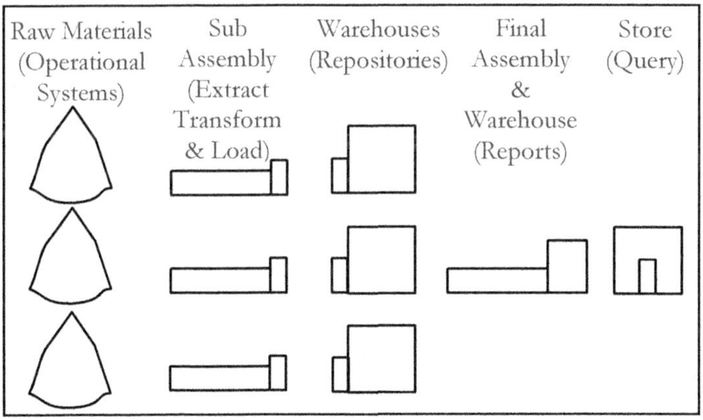

Figure 1 – The Data Warehouse Analogy

Chapter 3

OBSTRUCTIONS

Impediments to Accuracy, Completeness, Transparency, Timeliness, Availability, and Cost-Effectiveness

This description of how data flows is perhaps very familiar to those who work in this space; and although it brings improvements over cottage manufacturing processes before it, its limitations are quite evident.. There are some significant obstacles in our data flows. There is a nagging feeling that the answers we receive from the data aren't always accurate, if we are given the answer at all.

Many of the recent spectacular failures in business have been abetted by suspect data or misinterpretation of data. There is a sense that we should be able to avoid future economic problems because of all the data available.

Why can't we? One reason is a lack of **accuracy**; as copies of the data are created and move through the system, they often diverge, and often in significant ways. Thus, the answer provided in one report may be different to that provided in another. Which is right? It can be very difficult to determine.

A quality related to accuracy is **completeness**. That which is recorded may be accurate, but missing or incomplete data can be just as misleading as inaccurate data. And data might be missing because it was not captured, or it was lost in the flow from record to report.

A quality related to completeness is **transparency**, the ability to understand why an answer is so. When we don't understand the causes of problems, we focus our actions on the wrong drivers. This is because as data flows from raw material to the store, it becomes less connected to the customer or event; it is difficult to put them back together again. We understand the results in summary, like the profitability of the flight; we know *how* things stand, but not *why* because we lack the ability to "drill down" from the summary to the details. Which specific customer tickets were not profitable?

Another problem is a lack of **timeliness**. Just as it can take a long time for raw materials to be turned into manufactured goods, it can take a long time for data to move from the operational systems to the specific report or time period in some cases.

It can also be very difficult to find the answer to a question in the store. The answers simply are not **available**, because the data has not yet been converted into accessible, meaningful information.

Lastly, another problem with the entire system is high **costs**, those even beyond the opportunity costs mentioned above and those resulting from poor choices made due to unavailable, inaccurate, late, or misunderstood data. There are direct costs that are significant and growing.

When computers were invented, the amount of data they contained would have fit in a wheelbarrow, if not simply a bucket, and the percentage of total costs commensurate. Now data *is* a veritable mountain, and, despite continued advances in technology, the of associated cost trend lines are clearly rising faster than technology can reduce them. The costs of the computers, storage, staff, procedures, and processes are large enough; every time we make a copy of the data, we increase the costs.

Our needs for achieving increased accuracy, completeness, transparency, timeliness, and availability in more cost-effective ways will continue to drive changes in how data is stored and used. To understand these obstacles better, and how these changes are likely to evolve, we need to be more specific about how data is organized and copied.

Chapter 4

ORIGINS OF UNDERSTANDING

Transactions to Balances

Reporting is a process of gaining understanding: understanding how things are, why they are that way, what has happened or what might happen next, and how they might change. Reporting in business systems typically is not a narrative, like a newspaper article or this book. Rather, most often, it is a table—a spreadsheet— wherein we quantify things, with either counts or accumulated monetary amounts.

We learn how to quantify as children first by classifying, making different kinds of piles. We sort objects into piles by shape (round, long, or flat), size (large, medium, or small), and color (red, yellow, or blue). Objects that are flat, large, and red are placed in one pile, and objects that are yellow, medium-sized, and round in another.

True quantification comes next. The simplest report or table would show a count of the objects in each pile. The counts are simple metrics. A more advanced table would show the accumulated weight of all the objects in a pile. There might be some reports of counts and weights, but in business reporting, our reporting begins with and more frequently focuses on the *value* of the assets rather than the other potential characteristics.

ASSET TYPE	SUBTOTAL	TOTAL
Cash:		
Checking	238.95	
Savings	756.23	995.18
Investments:		
Stocks	6,239.98	
Bonds	2,596.21	8,836.19
Retirement:		
Pension	98,200.00	
401(K)	137,396.00	235,596.00
Cars		
Honda	8,456.04	
Ford	13,496.00	21,952.04
Home		220,456.21
Total Assets		487,835.62

Table 1 – Example Table of Balances

The summarized values in many business reporting tables—Total Assets and asset by type—are balances. They state how things stand right now, today, or for the period for which the balances were created. There may be many individual assets—many details behind these numbers—but the balances convey a great deal of meaning and information very simply and very concisely.

A balance of some kind typically conveys meaning very effectively. For this reason, the repository warehouses, final assembly lines, and stores of data contain many balances.

DATE	TRAN TYPE	ASSET CLASS	ASSET SUBCLASS	AMOUNT
Jan 1	Beg. Bal.	Cash	Checking	200.00
Jan 5	Deposit	Cash	Checking	43.21
Jan 23	Check	Cash	Checking	(4.26)
Jan 28	Transfer	Cash	Checking	(100.00)
Jan 1	Beg. Bal.	Cash	Savings	656.23
Jan 28	Transfer	Cash	Savings	100.00

Table 2 – Example Table of Transactions

We might think of the individual items in each pile as transactions. Transactions have limited usefulness by themselves, unless we want to know something specific (for example, the date we bought an asset). Balances are generally more useful, but transactions have greater completeness in representing what happened. Balances, by definition, summarize out details. Understanding begins with balances, and yet transactions are the "stuff" at the bottom of all balances.

As an example, suppose the cash balances in Table 1 were made from the transactions shown in Table 2. The first four transactions accumulate to the Checking Account ending balance of 238.95. Note that even here we have not shown all the transactions since the account was opened, instead using a "Beginning Balance" transaction to summarize transactions for prior days, months, years, or decades.

Our balances in Table 1 contain only two attributes, Asset Class and Asset Subclass, and an accumulated Amount. But our transactions in Table 2 contain two more columns, Date and Transaction Type. These two attributes are not available for reporting from our balances: they are characteristics we chose to ignore when making our piles. We would have to make other balances if we need to report on these attributes. Thus, because they hold additional attributes, transactions are more flexible for making reports, but they typically have to be made into balances before being really useful because most reporting starts with how things stand now—a balance—not how things changed—a transaction.

Is it possible to make a balance without accumulating transactions? Perhaps so. For example, you might inquire of an ATM machine what your account balance is without accumulating all the historical transactions, but this would be simply relying upon the bank's balance keeping. You could derive an inventory balance by counting a warehouse's inventory without regard to the receipts and shipments, but one might argue that the act of inventorying each item is a type of transaction and that the total amount on hand is a balance.[*]

Certainly we do not count the grains of wheat in a silo or the molecules in an oil tank. Imprecision in our measurements of transactions necessitates truing up totals at times. Yet even when truing up, we typically record the difference between what is on hand and our inventory record as a transaction called a *loss* or a *gain*. And without adding and subtracting transactions from balances between inventory counts, we would have no sense of where we stand. Balances are accumulations of individual items or transactions.

---

[*] Note that in some cases we use the term balance, as in a financial position, and we think we are referring to a transaction, but that's because the pile only contains one thing. The "balance owed" might be the same as a single, original transaction, because no incremental payment transaction was ever made.

ASSET TYPE	MONTH 1	MONTH 2
Cash:	995.18	723.48
Investments:	8,836.19	9,258.21
Retirement:	235,596.00	236,578.21
Cars	21,952.04	21,871.21
Home	220,456.21	220,456.21
Total Assets	487,835.62	488,887.32

Table 3 – Example of Balances by Month

Balances also represent copies of transaction data. As such they can contribute to the problems of accuracy, transparency, completeness, and so on. Let's examine how.

Suppose someone asks how assets changed over time. This requires us to make different piles of assets by type by time like that shown in Table 3. We list the type of assets and then a column for month 1 amounts and another for month 2 amounts, each column effectively being a different pile: One pile for how things were a month ago and another pile for how things are today. Yet we know that there really aren't multiple physical things in these "piles"; the house in pile 1 is probably the same house in pile 2. Yet we have made two copies of the transaction data.

This isn't a problem as long as everything is recorded properly and added correctly and never changes. But suppose we find that the listed value of the house was wrong—the data on the house transaction was incorrect. Of course, we can change the transaction. However, changing the transaction does not automatically change the balances that summarized this transaction. These copies of data are independent from the transaction.*

Correction isn't the only reason things change. At times, how we would record a transaction today is different from how we recorded it yesterday; we refine our meaning of the transaction or its value may simply change. For example, the home appraisal might now be higher. Yet again, these changes to a transaction or the creation of a new transaction do not change the corresponding balances.

A change to the home value affects at least six balances in our example tables, two on Table 1 and four on Table 3. All of these balances are floating around the organization, independent of the transaction, and all with the wrong value.

This impact to accuracy is real, and pervasive. Our ability—and need—to make copies of data in the form of balances to convey meaning is important. Yet we must find ways of making copies more accurate, making fewer of them, or perhaps linking them to transactions more closely by making temporary versions when needed.

---

* When (1) transactions and balances are stored in the same spreadsheet, (2) the formulas correctly associate transactions with balances, and (3) the spreadsheet is configured to automatically calculate after changes are made, the related balances can be updated "automatically." As well see, storing all data in one location, correctly specifying all these relationships, and applying the compute capacity to do that for larger amounts of data is impossible.

Chapter 5

CLARITY

Transparency, Traceability and Repeatability

Balances convey great meaning quickly about how things are, but they explain less clearly about *why* things are that way. We use transactions to create balances, yet the relationship is not just one way, from transactions to balances. Transactions (or more-detailed balances) often help explain a balance as we drill down from the balance to its constituent transactions.

In other words, transactions provide transparency.

Think of a bank account statement. The first number examined is the month-end balance. This balance quickly gives an overview of the status of things; whether the balance is small or large, we know where we stand.

Assume we did not use the account during the month. We would then expect little or no change in the balance. If the statement shows the same ending balance as the prior month, we need no detail; we already understand the balance.

If the balance changed unexpectedly, though, the only clue or cure—the only way to understand what happened—is to see more detail.

It may not require examining individual transactions initially. The statement might present summaries of total deposits and total withdrawals. These more-detailed balances may provide a clue to the problem and where to continue the investigation.

For example, if the summary of deposits is zero, we may immediately realize that our last deposit was just after the statement cutoff date and understand the reason for the unexpected ending balance.

If these more-detailed balances are not adequate, we may ultimately need the detailed transactions. We may need to find one significant transaction causing the balance to be very different than expected. It may be just one fraudulent, unrecorded, or forgotten transaction. Table 4 presents another example.

These needs extend from transparency to traceability and repeatability. Transactions prove that the balances are correct and that there have been no errors in addition or categorization. Traceability (the principle that all transactions that should be included have been and no others have been) and repeatability (accuracy in the aggregation mathematics) are required less frequently than transparency, but are perhaps more fundamental. They are related to the principles that we record things only once, that we designate systems of record for everything, and that we add correctly. Transparency is meaningless without confidence that the balance is fundamentally correct.

The process of tracing from balances to transactions is not neat and orderly in most large business systems. For example, some widely used balances summarize tremendous amounts of detail, like the net income for a multinational corporation. It summarizes all the income and expense transactions of the organization for an entire year. Drilling down from a single balance to a million or a billion detailed transactions actually provides no increased transparency; too many details do not enhance understanding.

Stocks	Beginning of Month	Net Change	End of Month
Balances:	$6239.98	$422.02	$6,662.00

Top of Statement: Balance Overview

Share Purchases	$4,251.07
Dividends	$193.44
Shares Sold	-$3897.69
Management Fees	-$124.80
Net Change:	$422.02

Case 1 Transaction Detail Report Section

Share Purchases	$4,251.07
Dividends	$193.44
Shares Sold	-$124.80
Management Fees	-$3897.69
Net Change	$422.02

Case 2 Transaction Detail Report Section

Suppose our statement contained the balances at the top of this report. If we remember we sold nearly $4,000 in shares, we may not need the case 1 transaction detail. If we did not sell shares, then the case 2 detail will be very important to understanding the ending balance.

Table 4 –Transparency Example

It is impractical to carry all the details with every balance. It would require making many copies of all the transactions because many balances summarize the same transactions. If we attempt to never store a balance but instead create it from the transactions when needed, we would consume huge amounts of compute capacity recreating balances each time they are needed.

We also can't simply infer what the details were for any balance. If we add two numbers together and store only the balance of 100, we can't guess which of the infinite possible combinations might have resulted in that value. Were the transaction amounts 23 and 77, or something else?

Is it not possible to maintain a link from the balance to the transactions? In some cases it is, if the balance involves limited sets of detail. Yet storing a link with the balance is often no different and just as voluminous as storing the details like 23 and 77, each requiring a unique key.

If we attempt to keep these links consistent and always accurate for all perspectives then given our current compute capacity, we would end up destroying the flexibility needed in the manufacturing line, transforming the entire environment into something like rock.

This point is worth emphasizing: Balances are used to manage compute capacity constraints, by not requiring recreation from transactions each time a balance is needed.

Through all our attempts to solve these problems, we are left needing ways of improving accuracy and transparency and yet live with the many capacity constraints of our systems today. This little dance of transaction to balances and back goes on over and over and over again in our quest to find meaning in the data.

In summary then, Transactions and Balances have the following characteristics:

TRANSACTIONS	BALANCES
Original records of business events[*]	Typically summaries of business events
Of limited usefulness for reporting by themselves, but very flexible for making reports, because:	The starting point for almost all reports, but limited for other uses because they are:
• Discrete events in time	• As of a point in time
• All attributes are available	• For a selected set of attributes
• All combinations are possible	• Answering a specific question
• All calculations are possible	• Typically simple aggregations

Balances have the following negative aspects:

- They duplicate the information stored on transactions (the real book of record)
- They are less flexible in reporting than transactions
- They require reconciliation to ensure confidence that they are correct
- If reconciled and in error, they require adjustment or the actions taken by the business could be wrong

---

[*] The world of Business Events is larger than the world of Transactions. A business event is anything the business wants to plan, execute, control, or evaluate—with financial impact or not—which may or may not be automated today as a transaction.

Balances are required because:

- They are the first step in reporting
- They show the status as of the current time, and
- They optimize resources needed to show that status going forward

Then the question becomes:

- Which balances to create and maintain
- When to create and maintain them
- How to create and maintain them

This ultimately becomes a question of optimizing computing resources.

Chapter 6

Posting And Reconciliation

The Original Business Systems

This relationship of balances and transactions was first documented by Luca Pacioli in the year 1494. After a few hundred years of performing the process manually, we applied computers to it in the same way we did it by hand.

This process is part of tens of thousands of computer applications, but is almost never talked about or considered directly. We might call it summarization or aggregation, but more appropriately, it is called *posting.*[*] Posting processes create balances, capturing the impacts of transactions over time.

First, we define what balances to make consistently, effectively selecting which characteristics or attributes of the transactions to track, like deciding which piles of things we should keep.

Then on a periodic basis (typically at the close of each business day), any new transactions since the last refresh of the balances are added or sent to the applicable balance. In other words, the program updates my account balance to reflect all my deposits

---

[*] This accounting sense of the word "to transfer or carry from a book of original entry to a ledger" may be related to the "publishing, announcing, or advertising," sense in that once the transactions are posted, the balance "announces" the current position. (Definitions from Merriam-Webster's 11th Collegiate Dictionary)

Last Night's Checking Acct. Balance		439.98
Today's Transactions:		
Gas purchased	-13.28	
Birthday toy purchased	-7.21	
Salary deposit	750.00	
Electric bill paid	-327.38	
Total movement in balance		402.13
This Evening's Checking Acct. Balance		842.11

Table 5 – Example Posting Process

and withdrawal transactions during the day. This is called "posting" the transactions to the corresponding balances in the "master file."* Table 5 shows an example.

Why do we do this? The simple answer is that it optimizes computing resources. Rather than using a posting process, each day we could produce all the balances needed for reporting for any time period using all the accumulated transactions from history. Doing so would minimize the need for reconciliation, because any new transactions—like any corrections or adjustments—would be included in the balances produced.

The problem with doing this is that the number of transactions required to produce balances over time continues to grow. A 20-year checking account requires 20 years of transactions to create today's balance. The compute capacity needed, whether

* Often this process can include creating a new copy of the balance file, the container for all the related balances, serving as a backup of yesterday's balances.

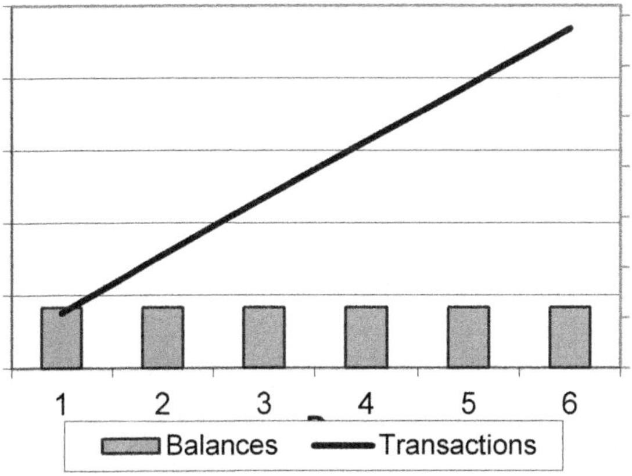

Graph 1 - Minimized Reconciliation

If transactions are used to produce every balance needed at report time, then the number of balances remain relatively constant—only those needed each day are created. However, the number of transactions required to make those balances increases over time because some balances require the inclusion of prior day transactions.

human brains 500 years ago or computers today, grows with each passing day.

If compute capacity continues to grow faster than transaction volumes, at some point perhaps creating balances may not be necessary.

Until then, though, using a posting process means that the prior balances and the incremental transactions from the last update create the new balances. The data volumes grow very little with time, thus compute capacity is stable. However, the downside of this approach is that any error in a balance for a

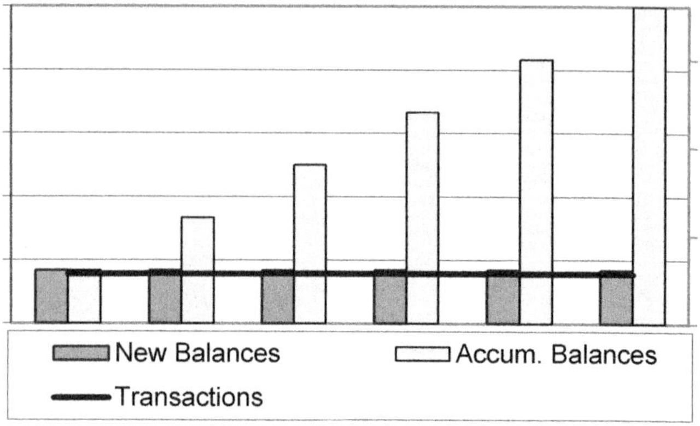

Graph 2 – Minimized Computing

Alternatively, if yesterday's balances are simply updated with today's transactions, the number of transactions each day remains relatively stable. However, the number of balances produced grows over time for historically comparative reports, and these balances must be reconciled to ensure accuracy.

particular time will not automatically be corrected. And because the transactions are the real record of business events, the balances must be tested against them to be sure they remain accurate. Thus instead of the transaction volumes growing to produce balances, the balances requiring reconciliation would continue to grow.*

Because compute capacity historically was very expensive, we started using posting processes to produce balances and lived

* The number of balances may grow at a slower rate than transactions, depending on the new types of analysis we desire which often require new balances.

with the inaccuracies that typically creep into the system. As compute cost have decreased, we have likely never considered an alternative approach.

This little posting process is ubiquitous. Inventory systems maintain inventory balances, updated as items are sold or materials are purchased or used. Payroll master files are updated as hours worked are recorded and payroll checks are created. These posting processes are examples of *operational systems*, the raw material mining processes for data. Even within the operational systems, we eliminate detailed transactions as quickly as possible to get to balances.

The chain of posting processes continues after the original operational systems. In some cases, the input "transactions" to subsequent posting processes are not business or operational events at all, like a deposit or withdrawal, but rather summarized transactions or even low-level balances from other operational systems.

The financial systems often receive these summarized inputs, representing the changes in balances from operational systems. An example would be a single "transaction" aggregating all the inventory changes for the day rather than one for each individual part or a total of all payroll payments made rather than one for each check written.

In large organizations, the layers of posting processes between some originating transactions and reporting balances may be half a dozen levels deep. By then, the transaction details are very far removed from the balances, with corresponding problems in accuracy and transparency.

Another problem shows up when we need to create balances to answer new questions. A posted balance—sometimes called a bucket, much like the child's pile—must be determined in advance. New balances cannot be easily created from scratch; the piles, like those for size and shape, are predetermined.

Suppose we didn't care about the object color when we made the piles. Yet now we ask about how many yellow items we have, and there is no pile containing just yellow things. The question requires inspecting each item. And since the transactions may be long gone, having been posted into the existing balance files and then archived, we have no way of getting the answer.

Could we create a balance file containing all the attributes of the transactions, every shape, color, and size? Technically yes, but practically it results in no summarization; it's as if we're keeping the transactions in the balance file. This is because a customer's deposit on a particular day at a particular time at a specific branch to a particular account would be summarized only with another transaction the same customer made at the same time on the same date at the same place. How many times would that happen! We would have (almost) as many balances as we have transactions.

Availability of the data to answer our questions is dependent upon someone having predicted our need for the answer and making a posting process to update a balance containing it. And since the types of questions we want to ask (thus changing the balances we need) are much more dynamic than the changes in the types of business events of organizations (which are recorded as transactions), we often ask questions which the balances don't support.

Chapter 7

PROLIFERATION

Duplicative Data Supply Chains

The ubiquity of posting processes in business may be driven in part by its antiquity. One can make a good case that the posting process was the first business application architecture, beginning with manual ledgers, then with punched cards as the transaction inputs, then with on-line entry screens.

The commonness is also due to their ease of implementation; it is not difficult to assemble a new team to create a new master file and posting process when a new type of analysis is needed.

The proliferation of these processes has been driven by the proliferation of attributes for which we want to report balances. Five hundred years ago, or even one hundred years ago, the financial system was the only set of balances maintained. Even banks and insurance companies use financial system-like processes to maintain balances. And because there were so few balances, reconciliation was not a major problem.

Yet consider our little personal balance sheet from Chapter 4. In that example, our transactions had four attributes in addition to the amount: Date, Transaction Type, Asset Class, and Asset Subclass. Those sample transactions created fourteen different balances if we include the subtotal. If all balances associated with every possible combination of attributes are of interest, then the number of possible balances would be the product of the number of values in each attribute.

DATE	TRAN TYPE	ASSET CLASS	ASSET SUBCLASS
Jan 1	Beg. Bal.	Cash	Checking
Jan 5	Deposit	Cash	Checking
Jan 23	Check	Cash	Checking
Jan 28	Transfer	Cash	Checking
Jan 1	Beg. Bal.	Cash	Savings
Jan 28	Transfer	Cash	Savings
Jan 3	Purchase	Invest.	Stocks
…	…	…	…
Total count of values for each attribute			
20	9	5	8

Table 6 – Counts of Attributes

Therefore, if the values in the last row of Table 6 show the number of values in each column, then the number of balances will be over 7,200 balances. There would need to be only about 600 transactions for these required unique combinations of attribute counts.*

This explosion of potential balances has given rise to thousands of posting processes in organizations. We are effectively attempting to create a balance (master) file for each attribute, like shape, color, and size, and each combination of attributes, like shape/color, shape/size, color/size, and shape/color/size. The same transactions are fed to multiple posting processes. In

---

* In our example, if Asset Class and Asset Subclass are truly a hierarchy, then not all permutations of balances may make sense.

other words, an object's color could update the color master file, then its size update the size master, then the shape update the shape master, a "transaction" being passed to three or more posting processes, each making copies of the transactions data.

We have stacked new posting processes on top of old ones, each taking in reduced volumes summarized by lower-level processes yet combining outputs from similar lower level systems and each providing a limited set of analytical results or reports. This has accommodated the growth in data volumes, analytics, and organizations, yet at the expense of more copies of data, greater need for synchronization, and less flexibility in the entire ecosystem.

At the bottom of the stack of processes, we might have 1,000 operational systems in large organizations. The outputs or transactions then feed perhaps 300 higher-level posting processes, like finance or risk, creating additional outputs. These 300 systems then feed 150 more analytical posting processes, like data warehouses and reporting applications. And so on up the posting process hierarchy we go, often losing detail all along the way.

The feeds from the operational systems typically flow to more than one higher-level posting processes, either in detail or in summary; the 1,000 systems have more than one "boss." For example, the finance system called the general ledger or GL accumulates all of the financial transactions from all of the originating source data systems. This is because it produces the financial statements for the organization, which require all financial transactions.

The general ledger isn't the only finance system gathering all the data from the source data systems. Quite often, the management accounting system does as well in some measure. In some highly regulated industries like financial services, the regulatory or statutory systems also collect data from the source data systems; these regulatory or statutory systems may also be owned by the finance department, but in a separate team from the general ledger system. More recently, risk systems have arisen, managed by a closely associated team. Then we have the customer analytic processes with their own growing appetite for all the source data, as well as related marketing systems. Operations also gets into the act, wanting to analyze cross-system implications. And on and on it goes.

Each separate reporting stream from source data systems to reports is a *data supply chain.*

Each is has sub-assembly lines with warehouses, leading to major manufacturing lines, holding duplicative data with numerous dependent analytical stores.

Each of these data supply chains requires nurturing and care and feeding and tending. They are fixed structures because the balances require consistent feeding to remain accurate. They become siloed, often diverging from the data contained in another flow. They are costly and inflexible.

Yet remember, the reason posting processes are used is to reduce the compute requirements of producing balances at a specific point in time. Different posting programs are required because the results need to be stored in different formats depending on the combination of attributes. In the case of our little sample table above, for example, the 7,200 balances would be in at most 10 different formats. Some of the balances would be simply the total balance of the transactions for a particular date, transaction type, or other attribute. Thus, they would have only one attribute. Others would be combinations of two attributes, others three, and others all four. The formula for calculating the possible structures is n(n+1)/2, with four attributes requiring 10 different layouts. In a modern company, there are hundreds of attributes, many with hundreds of possible values.

Pascal once wrote something like, "If I had more time I would have written you a shorter letter." This same sentiment is true when writing programs. Writing efficient programs takes a lot of time. And having created so many, over so many years, for so many different balances of different types means they are likely not tremendously efficient. Thus, the number of programs created undermines our use of posting programs to save compute capacity.

And that's not the only thing that has been undermined. More importantly, having so many of them undermines the credibility of the reports they provide. People know certain numbers on two different reports should be the same, even though they are produced by two different data supply chains. Yet often these numbers are different for very simple reasons.

For example, imagine you are reviewing a report that shows the total sales for a customer, and, by drilling down (that is, finding the detailed transactions which make up a balance) you see the sales for that customer for each product purchased. A number for a specific product here should be the same as that found in a report that is sorted and summarized first by product and then by customer. Quite often, these two numbers are not the same because of differences in the separate posting processes. This fact undermines the credibility of both reports and the processes that created them. Table 7 on the next page shows this example.

A basic cause of the differences may be that the posting processes do not post every transaction. The balances to be produced by one posting engine may be more narrowly defined, and thus only subsets of transactions are actually included in that summary. This selection logic is hidden from subsequent uses of the posted balance.

We can see the results of the transactions that *were* posted to the balance file, but not the ones that were *not* posted. Only by comparing to another complete balance file can we detect missing transactions. This incompleteness is one simple cause of discrepancies between different supply chains.

This comparison is a reconciliation process, and we need more of these with the multiplication of duplicative data supply chains.

Reconciliation is easier if both systems speak the same "language" making the comparison simpler. However, the different data supply chains often use different "languages" and code sets as we aggregate from one geography or business unit to another. Imagine what is lost in translation.

What is the cost of this proliferation? It's hard to say in total, but the numbers are likely substantial. Consider how we overcome the need for transparency with just our existing processes, by manually running the computer backwards:

Someone guesses at the transactions from the source data system for some balance and then dumps this to a spreadsheet. They then make subtotals of various rows and try to recreate the balance. Having finally recreated the balance on the report in the spreadsheet, that person is ready to begin the analysis of the transactions to understand why the balance is what it is. This manual process is performed over, and over, and over again in today's organizations.

There must be a better way.

Report 1:
Sales by Customer by Product

Customer: ABC Corp		
Product A	150.00	
Product B	80.00	
Product C	300.20	
Total Customer, ABC Corp		530.20

Report 2:
Sales by Product by Customer

Product: A		
Customer ABC Corp	155.00	
Customer DEF Corp	200.00	
Customer GHI Comp.	133.21	
Total Product, A		488.21

A user should expect either 150.00 or 155.00 in both reports covering the same period for Customer ABC and Product A. Perhaps they differ because the reports are from two different balance files, the 155.00 including additional transactions totaling 5.00. Greater transparency is necessary to explain the difference.

Table 7 – Example Report Discrepancy

Chapter 8

TIME ZONES AND CLOCK SPEEDS

The Periodicity of Reporting

Computers are amazingly fast at certain tasks when compared to humans. And they have continued to become faster year after year. But they do have limits, and how quickly some limits are reached can be quite surprising.

A funny thing happened while putting all these posting processes in place: we stopped thinking about how to improve posting, how and if innovation was possible. Few have seriously considered if changes might produce dramatic benefits in reporting results and better intelligence.

Given the great speed of computers, why should we make balances at all? Computers are very efficient at adding things up, repeatedly. If balances are copies of data and disconnected from the details, then why make them? Said another way: when adding up a set of numbers, one has the answer before writing it down. Why can't computers display or print the answer, without storing the balance, and do that again the next time someone asks?

Effectively if we had unlimited computing capacity, why would we ever store balances? The answer is we would not.

Even if we had to recreate totals from the past, we could do this by simply including date and time as part of a selection of which transactions to accumulate; in other words, we could have the computer select only the original transactions used to calculate the balance.

Although all of this is theoretically possible with today's technology, barring a major technical breakthrough, it still isn't practical. The reason is that computers are just not fast enough. The growth in computer speeds and capacities can generally keep up with the growth of data, but probably not with the growth in the types of analyses we desire, the answers to our new questions.*

We need to understand why, but to keep from becoming too technical here, let's simplify the computer in our discussion to three parts: CPUs, memory, and disk. Let's think of it like a meeting in a conference room, with people, a whiteboard, and a binder of agendas and meeting minutes.

In our meeting, people do the thinking, meaning that only they "understand" data, select the right rows, sort them, and add things up. They are the CPUs.

They work primarily with the whiteboard, because it is visible to all and allows things to change very quickly. The whiteboard is memory. Memory and whiteboard space are very fast, but limited.

That is where the binder comes in; it stores the results when they overflow the whiteboard, or during meeting breaks. There is much more space in the binder, but it is much slower to use.

---

* Dan Aminoff noted, "If the analysis requires sparse access then this is possible – e.g., billions of people can ask for many different things using Google, and the answers can be found across exabytes of data in milliseconds. Since the various economies change at varying rates, it's conceivable much of what today is done with balances could be more efficiently done by keeping all transactions at some point." (Note to Author)

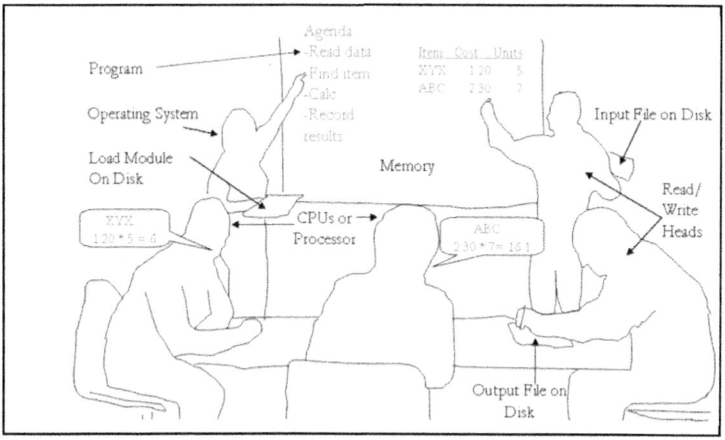

Figure 2 –Computer Analogy

It takes a long time to put the binder data on the whiteboard, or to record the results of work back in the binder.

The scarcity of memory, the slowness of disk, and the transfers required between them has historically significantly affected reporting processes. But even the speed of processors—the amount of work they can perform each second—is limited and can at times become the problem.

There is one more principle we need to consider. It is time and how it affects the entire system.

Since the earliest days of accounting and continuing into the age of computing, the quantity of data has always exceeded the compute capacity available to do everything with the detail. Yet the use of posting processes to create balances has provided pragmatic ways to overcome this limitation, producing the analyses we have today.

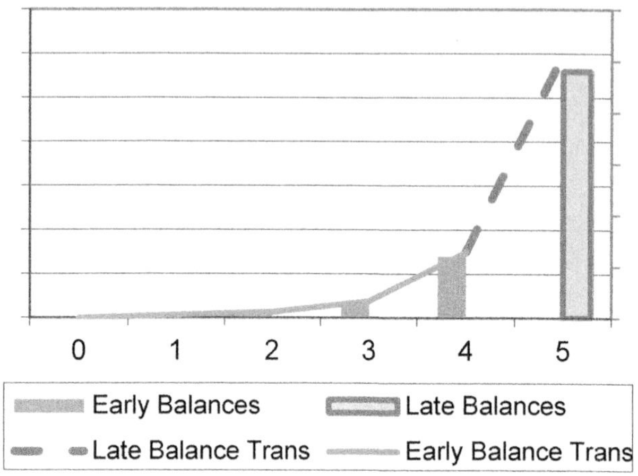

Graph 3 – Balances by Attribute Combinations

If the x-axis is the number of attributes needed to produce a balance, the number of possible combinations of attributes (and thus resulting balances) likely grows with each new attribute. At some point, the compute capacity limits production of some balances. Balances requiring more attributes are then produced later when more compute capacity becomes available.

Our pragmatism begins by never producing all balance permutations; we deem some combinations of attributes as providing little insight. Others are designated as critical or time-sensitive and are used to manage businesses very directly. Although limited in number because of compute capacity constraints, we produce them every morning by perhaps 8 AM (or earlier for demanding users).

Because these critical balances contain only a subset of the possible attributes of interest (as all balances do), we produce the additional, more detailed balances later, again reusing the

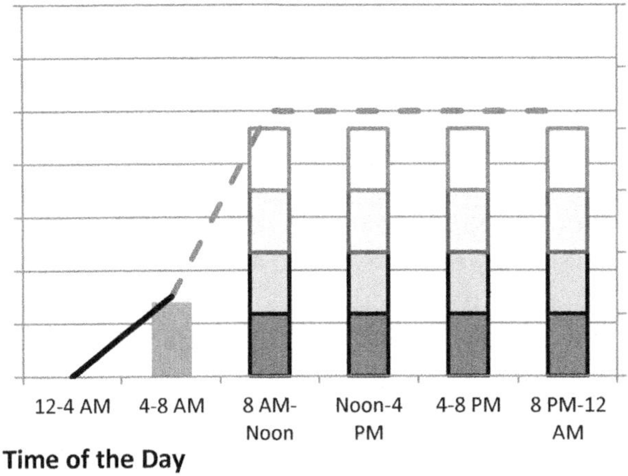

Graph 4 – Typical Daily Processing Cycle

The compute capacity constraint means that balance creation processes must be prioritized; critical balances, like those required by finance, must be created before 8 AM. Other functional areas come later, like risk, MI, regulatory, and customer analytics. This is a primary cause of duplicative data supply chains. The balances are produced at different times, using different aggregations of transactions, and thus do not reconcile. New balances cannot be created because the appropriate transaction details have been lost.

transactions in separate processes. This is the point of divergence in data supply chains: The critical balances, and then everything else. And "everything else" is typically judged by its agreement to the crucial balances—a judgment made through reconciliations.

Note that we measure computer speeds in instructions per second, cycles for a period, or gigahertz: all measures of time.

Also, note that balances also have a time aspect to them: They summarize results for a period.

This time aspect to balances creates a periodicity in reporting or, at least, balance creation. In other words, a large part of reporting is analyzing what happened over time. And that reflection, that analysis, is periodic, removed most often by at least some time from the last transaction. Certainly the periods between analyses shorten as the pace of business increases, moving from yearly to quarterly to monthly, and are getting shorter. Yet balance creation still happens periodically.

When more frequent analysis is needed, the limited number of transactions since the last posting process can be added to the last balance to create a temporary balance. Doing so is possible because the transactions are limited by the interval between postings.

A daily frequency for a single location, it seems, is the most likely frequency we will settle on for most balance build posting processes.[*] Shorter cycles will typically remain in the operational area or required only on certain days of the month.

As explained in the next section, the alternative to this historical approach is to produce many more detailed balances, but not every permutation, during the critical balance run. Said another way, produce more detailed balances *for a limited set of attributes* on a daily basis, yet maintain the linkage to the other attributes of interest. This approach allows a single highly tuned process to produce these balances. These more detailed balances can then be combined to produce the more aggregated balances needed later in the day. Doing so reduces reconciliation because the more detailed balances are fully

---

[*] As we will see shortly if these balances are stored as movements, then these daily balances can be accumulated into balances for longer periods.

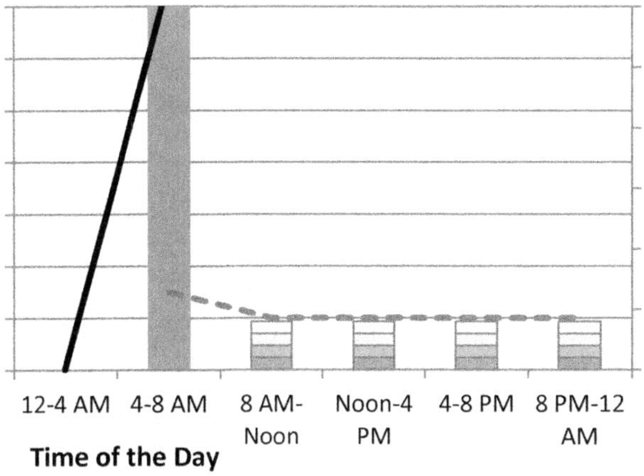

Graph 5 – Detailed Balances with Pivot to Alternatives

Alternatively, if many more detailed balances—including all business critical balances—were produced by start of day, then permutations of these balances could be produced later, and yet all would reconcile, having been produced from the same transaction details.

reconciled. This is a radically different approach than what we have done with posting processes for hundreds of years.

This daily process, though, shouldn't be taken for granted. I have witnessed numerous projects where trying to accomplish on a daily basis what historically was done on a monthly basis became very difficult; cases where processes which needed to finish in a couple of hours in the morning required more than 24 hours (and at times 50 to 60 hours) to complete. The periodicity of reporting can be very demanding.

Some people working on these problems chose to define their solutions as not being subject to the relentless demands of the clock,: saying that they were building *informational* not *operational* systems. Perhaps the lack of timeliness could be excused at that time, but our need for better information demands more innovation. The next evolution in reporting is recognizing that informational systems must take on more operational characteristics.

What's required is focusing on system performance—a near single minded focus on performance—to significantly reduce the time required for posting and aggregation processes.

This doesn't require a major innovation in computer technology. Even now, we can use time to our advantage. We can use this daily cycle of half the world being dark to organize the data for a designated geography. This organization of the data, along with enhancing the scalability of the posting process and moving it closer to the time of report production, can remove the obstructions to more accurate and timelier analytics, with a greater level of transparency and availability and at sustainable levels of cost.

Manufacturing systems have changed a lot since the first assembly lines were created. Perhaps it is time our measurement systems caught up. Let's consider how we might apply more recent innovations in manufacturing to the world of quantitative analytics to make a metric engine.

Chapter 9

JIT MANUFACTURING

Just-In-Time Analysis

Auto manufacturers invented the assembly line over a century ago. To set up an assembly line, one must determine specifically what output to produce—which type of vehicle, for example—and then configure the line to produce that output.

One challenge with this model is that it depends upon forecasting demand for the outputs. If these projections are wrong, then either potential sales are lost or surplus goods are produced. The costs can be substantial.

Posting processes are similar to these assembly lines. We configure systems to produce the balances before we turn them on, and once turned on the posting processes cannot produce other types of balances; we produce balances (and reports) no one cares about any longer and likely we don't produce the new balances needed to solve today's problems.

More recently, a new production strategy called just-in-time manufacturing was devised. Rather than producing and holding completed goods, workers configure the assembly line to hold components closer to raw materials in an organized way so that at the receipt of an order, the line produces that specific unit. This reduces the risk associated with forecasting. Personal computer makers were leaders in this approach.

A similar approach could be applied to report balance creation. Our assembly line would use data closer to the transaction-like raw materials and assemble balances much closer to when they are actually requested or needed.

Yet for analysis requiring more than hundreds of thousands of transactions, we cannot simply keep the transactions in their raw form on the assembly line. Today's balance assembly line—today's computer resource—is sized for today's workload. The volume of the transactions produced over many days would overwhelm it, and with our current systems, the cost of massive new capacity is difficult to justify.

This isn't much different from just-in-time PC manufacturing. PC lines don't begin with raw materials like silicon for CPUs, petroleum for plastics, and raw copper for wiring. It isn't necessary to go to the extreme for ultimate flexibility. The CPUs, optical disk readers, and graphics cards are subassemblies manufactured (perhaps at third-party suppliers, with their own just-in-time assembly processes) prior to arriving at the main line.

The manufacturing process for balances does have to change from our historical approach. Just-in-time manufacturing means we are attempting to eliminate the warehouse as much as possible, and the subassemblies have to be more flexible to be used in many more configurations.

So what would these subassemblies look like for our balance build processes? I propose that the equivalent in balance manufacturing is to make the first-level posting process produce just daily changes in balances at a much lower level of detail than the balances we have made historically. Doing so opens up follow-on innovations.

Rather than summarizing away all details, maintaining daily changes in balances for something like an individual customer/contract or vendor/contract combination provides tremendous flexibility in subsequent aggregations. Producing these balances eliminates the initial need for many of the more detailed transactions, and yet does not destroy as many of the attributes of potential interest to those who would "order" manufactured balances of various types.

Most questions asked outside the operational systems do not begin with questions about specific customer or account transactions. Rather, they are about various aggregations of many customers and the combinations of accounts or contract details. Thus we can eliminate detailed transactions through these low-level postings. Transparency may require drill-down to specific customers, but answers typically begin as aggregations.

In summary, our "assembly line" needs a way to accept a request (similar to an order for a new PC) and then manipulate these detailed prefabricated balances to create the requested balance. Doing so efficiently can be very challenging. We must use time zone windows very effectively to prepare the components from the raw materials and put them on the assembly line, and then manufacture the balance so that the user is not waiting too long.

Chapter 10

THE METRIC ENGINE

Trusted, Aggregated, Structured Data

Search engine technology has developed rapidly over the last decade and a half. It is an assembly line for a slightly different kind of answer than a quantitative metric. It has raced ahead of the older and more slowly developing posting engines.

Search engines provide aggregated views of tremendous amounts of qualitative (not quantitative), textual (not numeric) information, aggregated in the sense that we often find the answer to our question in the search result listings without drilling into the details. Yet they are less useful for quantitative analysis. Consider these questions:

When was the last time you entered a number into a search term, except for an address or a year? It is likely not recently. We typically search textual, not numeric, data in an Internet search engine[*].

Have you ever wondered about the quality of the results to these searches? Largely, search engine results are information

---

[*] An exception is the Wolfram Alpha search engine, at www.wolframalpha.com, which encourages searching for quantitative data. However, this engine is not intended to accumulate large amounts of transactional data to produce a balance.

	Textual Qualitative Unstructured Information	**Numeric Quantitative Structured Information**
High Value	Most Audited Footnotes to Financial Statements	Most Audited Financial Statements Tables
Moderate or Unknown Value	Some Personal and Opinion Blogs	Some Market Research and Business Plan Projections

Figure 3 – Quality and Types of Information

people give away freely, or perhaps sell at advertising rates, probably not the highest value data.

Lastly, what was the structure of the information returned by the search engine? It mostly tends to be unstructured data. The words on this page are unstructured. Structured data, on the other hand, tends to look much more like the columns and rows in a table or a spreadsheet.

The amount of structured data—data in spreadsheets—not released on the Internet likely dwarfs the structured data which has been released in both quantity and value. This is because the majority of structured data is deemed to be high value; companies promise customers that they won't release it and governments mandate they don't.

So if Internet search engines aggregate largely unstructured, textual, qualitative information, much of moderate value, what processes aggregate quantitative, high value, structured data?

The answer, of course, is posting engines, the systems built and maintained inside organizations for decades now, some of the oldest systems in business, like the general ledger systems. They are the bedrock of the capital markets. Are the numbers they produce relevant in today's world? Just consider what happens every time earnings by an actively traded company are released. The quantitative results move the market, affecting trillions of dollars every day.*

Why haven't companies simply applied an internal search engine to this problem? The primary reason has been aggregation. Aggregation produces balances. The assembly line for a search engine has not included this step. Could it include this step? Certainly. Will it? That remains to be seen.

To date, a search engine typically presents each occurrence—each "transaction" if you will—individually. An Internet search of a common term with billions of occurrences will show each occurrence if we click "Next" long enough, but aside from the count of returned results, nowhere can we see the accumulated impact of all those occurrences.

Additionally, by its nature quantitative data isn't easily digestible by search engines. Imagine a search engine result-page showing row after row of data from a spreadsheet. How useful is that?

Yet in spite of these differences, this more recently developed search engine manufacturing process can perhaps help us understand possible new approaches to quantitative analysis. Let's drill down on its steps of production to see if innovation in quantitative analysis—creation of a metric engine—is possible.

---

* Admittedly, this highly summarized, quantitative information is released and found on the Internet and in many search results.

Chapter 11

GATHERING TRANSACTIONS

Supply Chain Part 1

Let's compare and contrast textual and numeric data supply chains—the manufacturing processes for qualitative and quantitative analytics.

First off, consider the evolution that occurred early within the Internet search engine data supply chains: Many of the first, large search engines were really directories, maintained by people. People would find interesting web sites and categorize them in a hierarchical structure of topics. It did not take long before growth in data volumes forced them to abandon attempting to impose an organized hierarchy of answers to predefined questions.

In the quantitative world, in some respects we are still using directories. Our predefined posting engines produce one type of answer: the summary-level posted outputs defined at system startup time. How would we move away from directories to automated search engines?

Automated Internet search engines (as opposed to search directories) begin manufacturing the material that will be used to generate answers by ingesting and organizing raw data. They do this through something called spiders or crawlers, which access web pages periodically and take a copy of the data to add to the search engine database. They organize the inputs instead of trying to predict the questions.

This approach makes sense for quantitative analytics as well. What changes in business organizations more rapidly, the types of analysis we do or the types of business transactions—better termed *business events*—we undertake? The answer is that analyses change much more rapidly. The vast majority of the core operational functions have changed little over the last decade and in some industries over the last 50 or more years. The technology might have changed, as with the introduction of the Internet, but the types of business transactions, particularly those with financial implications, for the most part are very stable.

It is much simpler to organize the input for analytical processes than to anticipate the potential outputs that will be required from them.

Today's posting process have spider- and crawler-like equivalents to gather the details. In recent times we've called them *Extract/Transform/Load* (or ETL) processes. Earlier systems, particularly financial systems, had components called *Accounting Rules Engines* (or AREs), performing similar functions for financial transactions.

As we've noted, quantitative analysis normally deals with fixed reporting periods, and, as a result, puts more demands on the supporting infrastructure than text search does. If I make an update to my web page, but a search engine web crawler doesn't access it for a week and update the search database, search results may be out-of-date for a few days, but would be fine once the database was updated. If, on the other hand, I am measuring daily sales for each store and looking for trends over time, then accumulating two days' worth of sales into one day's balance would certainly skew my analysis from that point forward.*

The search engine's capture of the web pages could be thought of as a snapshot of how things look at one point in time; how the web page looks when the web crawler accessed it. On the metric side, it is also possible to pull "snapshots" as well, and some systems do this to save time and expense in construction and storage. They extract the accumulated *balances* in the source data system and ignore the transactions. For example, the checking account system holds the end-of-day balance for that account as well as each check and deposit transaction.†

Having only snapshot-based metrics limits the types of analysis we can do. For example, the end-of-day balance tells me nothing about the activity in that account throughout the day. If I made a $1,000,000 deposit and wrote checks for that same amount, my end-of-day balance would be the same as the prior day. When compared to the account for another customer who had no transactions on that day, my account would look the same. That missing information is critical for many metric analyses.

Thus, our system, to answer a broader set of questions, should pull transactions, not snapshots.‡ These transactions can be used to track balances that are not netted like many source data

---

* A sophisticated quantitative posting engine can backdate transactions to the appropriate period no matter when they are presented for posting; many systems are not able to do this in an easy or comprehensive manner.

† These balances are updated through a posting process in the operational system

‡ Accounting rules engines (AREs) typically use transactions: Journal entries are representations of transactions.

Contract ID	Transaction Type	Date	Amount
A75234	Fees Paid	Jan 3	(3.45)
34985	Buy	4-1	-341.32
5674	Sold	5 January	310.21

Original Transactions

Contract ID	Transaction Type	Date	Amount
3	Fees Paid	January 3	-3.45
4	Shr. Purchase	January 4	341.32
5	Shr. Sold	January 5	-310.21

Translated Transactions

The top three rows show originally recorded transactions. Note that dates, contract IDs, and even amounts are not recorded in the same manner. These transactions can be conformed to a common language in the translated transactions.

Table 8 – Translation to Common Langauge

system balances, or subject to other shortcuts for the convenience of the source data system.

A final point on this data sourcing process: The term "Transform" in ETL means "translate into a common language." To aggregate data and produce a measurement, it must be in the same language or code set. If we want to know the total balance for a single banking customer who has a credit card, checking account, and mortgage, the customer ID used to aggregate the records must be the same on all three records.

If the checking account is stored as "Hello," our search engine would not automatically find the associated mortgage stored as "Hola," the Spanish greeting. Search engines can translate outputs upon request, but they typically don't translate inputs. Metric engines must translate inputs to be useful.

Metric engines must do this because we can't afford the translation time for all the required transactions when manufacturing an answer. And translation isn't just a problem between countries; even within the same country typically each source data system uses a different "language" to record its transactions. If we don't put them into a common language, we won't be able to aggregate the transactions to get to a balance for the customer or for other report attributes later.

This translating process may have aspects of what some call "data cleansing." Data cleansing or clean-up must be done carefully; as in antiques, what is one man's grime is another's patina. We have to get to consistency in order to create balances, but destroying the originating data in the process can inhibit the value of analysis available.

A related point is determining when to adjust data. In some cases, data is known to be incomplete or even wrong. Again, when adjusting, it is best to enter adjustments as new business events or transactions, which allows questions on original values and adjusted values to be answered.

How to determine what to cleanse or to adjust? Both are like cleaning a room. The first step in cleaning is to turn the light on, and turning the light on in data systems means reporting on it. Exposing the data through reporting of some kind will facilitate more data cleansing than any other approach.*

So our data preparation processes will have some of the same basic functions, but will also be different in some respects. Now, let's consider the next leg of the supply chain: creating the low-level balances. This is the next step in the manufacturing process.

* Perhaps the closest analogy in the Internet search world is the "data cleansing" required by mandate for search engines not to show some types of harmful or sensitive web pages.

Chapter 12

LOW-LEVEL POSTING

Data Supply Chain Part 2

So we've gathered, translated and organized the transactions, but we've agreed rather than just use transactions we require the use of many aggregates that accumulate over time, showing the impact over months and years. To efficiently use compute resources and not have to recalculate the balance from last year's transactions before getting to today's balance, we must perform some level of posting process in the metric and balance-based data supply chain.

Here we diverge from the Internet assembly line analogy quite dramatically for the next step, because creating balances is a step that search engines do not do. So although the data preparation in the prior chapter and the final aggregation in the next chapter have analogous components in the search engine world, this aggregation step is unique to metric engines.

This step allows us to use lower compute capacities, because balances show a position without having to manipulate all the transactions from the beginning of time. Doing this step correctly will dramatically enable quantitative analytics.

We've found that balances by themselves present challenges when the data gathering process isn't flawless. For example, if data wasn't gathered from a source three days ago and balances have been made each day since, the correction process involves more than just correcting the balance from three days ago; each

Row ID	Record Type	Balance Date	Amount
1	Balance	January 1	1,020.00
2	Balance	January 2	1,020.00
3	Balance	January 3	1,030.00
4	Balance	January 4	1,030.00
5	Balance	January 5	1,022.44

Balance Table

Row ID	Movement Type	Movement Date	Amount
6	Opening Bal	January 1	1,020.00
7	Dividends	January 3	10.00
8	Fees Paid	January 5	-7.56

Movement Table

The first table above shows pure balances, whereas the second table shows movements. We can calculate any value in the first from the data in the second. If we receive row 7 for posting after row 8, we must update rows 3, 4 and 5 if balances are kept. If we calculate balances dynamically from movements, we need no updates.

Table 9 – Movement Example

subsequent day's balance must also be corrected. Our computer capacity may allow for three days of reprocessing, but likely not 23 days.

An easy solution is to avoid making true balances; we can instead post accumulated changes in balances each day, creating something called a *summary movement*. This simplifies the update problem, requiring only one value to be changed when transactions requiring backdating are encountered. However, this also moves a portion of the work from this phase to the final aggregation phase. We will have to aggregate these summarized movements to arrive at the final balance.*

Daily changes in balances provide very flexible building blocks (manufactured subassemblies) for most of our time dimensions. They can be accumulated to longer periods, used to calculated averages, added together to show a position at many points in time, and easily updated for backdated processing.

But what are the classifying attributes of the balances we need? Something has to describe what the balance is for: the yellow, flat, skinny types of attributes. The attributes typically are a subset of the attributes of the source transactions, so let's start there.

Transactions often have something like a time stamp, which usually will not aggregate with any other transaction to make a balance. Even if we step back from this extreme case, some attributes aggregate so little that we will effectively have transactions even with aggregation, and we can't use transactions because the data volumes would grow too large. This leads us to drop some uniqueness in the aggregating attributes. So in creating balances, there will likely be some transaction attributes our assembly line will not have readily available for downstream analysis without going back to the original transactions.

---

* Throughout the remainder of this discussion, we will use the words balance and movement interchangeably, whether referring to a true balance or an accumulated change (i.e., summarized movement) in a balance.

Fund ID	Fund Name	Risk Type	Date Purchased
1	Fund A	Aggressive	1998
2	Fund B	Aggressive	2001
3	Fund C	Moderate	1998

Mutual Fund Attribute Tables

Fund ID	Balance/Trans -action Type	Balance Date	Amount
1	Opening Bal	January 1	1,020.00
1	Dividends	January 3	10.00
1	Fees Paid	January 5	-7.56
2	Opening Bal.	January 1	378.00
3	Opening Bal	January 1	737.32
3	Fees Paid	January 3	-3.45

Low-level Balance or Transaction Table

We could store the "Date Purchased" on each balance, but Fund ID 1 in the bottom table would have "1998" duplicated on each row. By using the Fund ID, we can link these two records together when needed.

Table 10 –Balance Attribute Example

We therefore must choose which attributes will have a running balance (or movement) kept for them and which will be accessible only on transactions. A balance for any attributes not kept as a running balance will require transaction accumulation, literally recalculating from details*.

Understanding the resolution to this conundrum of how to organize the data is at the heart of the solution to our current problems. This requires us to consider a rather technical subject called data modeling. Let's see if we can make this subject a little more approachable.

The solution might be informed by what we do in the operational systems. Source data systems typically hold individual daily contract or product balances. This level maintains access to all the attributes for customer, contract, and product, yet does not place those attributes on each balance; we don't burden the source data system low-level posting processes with all those attributes. See Table 10.

For example, we may know that a customer's mortgage interest rate is 5%. We could duplicate this value, recording it on every transaction, every payment, every interest amount calculation, every transaction—but why? It would simply duplicate the same data over and over again. Storing the data only once is called *normalizing* the data. Not doing so is called *denormalizing*.

In the search engine world, we denormalize the data in a sense. We require all the words we want to search for to be on the same webpage, even if this causes duplication of data on more detailed pages for things like the company name. But doing so on structured transactional data will expand the data volumes significantly.

---

* Alternatively, we could actually choose to maintain multiple summary structures that require reconciliation; maintaining two *reconciling* data supply chains is still much less expensive than maintaining ten.

Rather than keeping these same attributes on each balance, we could instead store the customer contract ID, a single value that is repeated on each balance identifying it as this specific customer's mortgage. We could then use this identifier to "join" the balances to all the associated contract attributes, like interest rate, when needed.

Joining is a very simple exercise of finding one record's "key" or unique identifier value on another record. We manually join data when we use the phone number from the phone bill and search for the corresponding name in our contact list. Thus, the phone number "key" in a way gets us to all the other attributes of the person. See Table 11.

So we need a key for the customer or vendor and for the contract/product attributes. Along with this key, the other attributes needed to classify the low-level balances are remarkably few. Low-level balances can be summarized by time period (typically a day), currency (transaction, functional, reporting), company (legal entity, the company that owns the balance), a type (something like a general ledger account will often suffice, such as revenue, cost, type of expense, principal, fees, and so on) and a few other attributes.

We can maintain the customer, vendor, contract, and product details on separate structures, and link from these to the low-level balances, through the permanent identifier or a key that does not change, such as a customer-contract-product number.

Let's use another simple example, as shown in the Tables 14 and 15 at the end of the chapter. Suppose you hold multiple mutual funds, each with a risk designation—aggressive, moderate, or conservative—and you want (1) a report of the balances in your mutual funds by risk and, (2) a report by date purchased. We could create two posting processes for two separate master files, one for each report. Every time you buy

Fund ID	Fund Name	Risk Type	Date Purchased
1	Fund A	Aggressive	1998

Mutual Fund Attribute Tables

Fund ID	Balance/Trans-action Type	Balance Date	Amount
1	Opening Bal	January 1	1,020.00
1	Dividends	January 3	10.00
1	Fees Paid	January 5	-7.56

Low-level Balance or Transaction Table

Fund Name	Risk Type	Date	Balance Amount
Fund A	Aggressive	January 5	1,022.44

Temporary Reporting Record

We can combine the top four records in memory (the bottom three needed to change movements to a true balance) to temporarily create the last record for reporting.

Table 11 – Join Example

or sell a mutual fund, pay a management fee, or receive a dividend, we accumulate the balances by the risk in one file and by date purchased in another file.

Alternatively, we could have one balance file with the mutual fund key, and a separate mutual fund attribute table with the same key. This second table doesn't contain any transaction amounts or balances, just attributes describing the mutual funds, like risk designation and mutual fund purchase date.

Thus, this file isn't updated in the posting process and doesn't require reconciliation.

To manufacture our reporting balances, we can combine these two tables, or join them, temporarily bringing these records together with all the fund attributes and the balances. Yet we never store this record, keeping the balances independent of the reporting attributes that need them.

We use this temporary record like a transaction to aggregate to both reports. Doing so produces two different reports off of one single data supply chain. We have only one posting process maintaining the low-level balances. Producing two outputs from one posting table starts the process of consolidating data supply chains.

One additional enhancement: Let's make our key to the attribute table include the effective date for the attributes—the date this set of attributes took effect. For example, by adding a new record whenever the risk attribute changes and specifying which date to use in the join, we increase even further the number of potential outputs from the same set of data. This includes the ability to reproduce reports from a prior (or even future) point in time because the computer puts the data back together as it was (or will be) at that point in time. (Table 12)

Let's consider one more aspect to the low-level posting process. We've discussed the need to translate attributes into a common language to allow aggregation. There may also be a need to translate the amounts on our records as well, so that they can be aggregated. For example, if a balance attribute for a mortgage payment in the US contains "Mortgage-Pay" and in Brazil it is "Hipoteca-Pagamento", obviously those two attributes will need to be translated into a common value if we wish to accumulate the balances associated with each. However, if the US Mortgage Payment is denominated in US

Fund ID	Effective Date	Fund Name	Risk Type
1	January 1	Fund A	Aggressive
1	January 4	Fund A'	Moderate

Mutual Fund Attribute Tables

Fund ID	Balance/Trans -action Type	Balance Date	Amount
1	Opening Bal	January 1	1,020.00
1	Dividends	January 3	10.00
1	Fees Paid	January 5	-7.56

Low-level Balance or Transaction Table

Fund Name	Risk Type	Date	Balance Amount
Fund A	Aggressive	January 1	1,020.00
Fund A'	Moderate	January 5	1,022.44

Temporary Reporting Record

The first temporary record is joined as of the 1st of January, but the second is as of the 5th, using the Mutual Fund attributes effective beginning the 4th

Table 12 – Effective DateExample

Dollars, and the Brazilian in Reals, the aggregated balance will be meaningless. We can't add Dollars and Reals and get a meaningful metric.

The process of getting these values into a common base is called *multi-currency processing* (see Table 13 and the appendix). Performing this and similar functions, requires us to generate new transactions showing the values in the selected common currency. The number, diversity, and complexity of these similar processes shouldn't be underestimated. They might include allocation processes which divide our metrics into smaller units and assign them to other owners; transfer pricing, which determines what something costs when there is no natural market; and consolidation and elimination processes, which identify particular transactions for inclusion or exclusion in reporting processes.

Because of the volume of data and processing requirements involved, these processes would typically be performed as part of the low-level posting processes. In some cases they require the business event transactions be applied first, and then these functions are performed on the resulting balances; in other cases, they may be done on the individual transactions and then the results accumulated. These processes are a bit like creating new transaction systems using the originating transaction systems as input.

All of this work we've described could be thought of as a subassembly process, something like preparing CPUs, hard disks, and video cards before the main assembly process for the PC.

The process of preparing these components then looks like this:

1. Prepare the customer contract attribute file, updating or inserting new rows as attributes describing customers, contracts, and products change. These structures typically do not entail amounts in need of posting.
2. Translate transactions into a common language or code set because each operational system will typically have its own code set and data structures.
3. Post transactions to make the needed low-level balances with the consistent key noted, and store the summary movements on a daily basis.

Currency	Date	Rate	Change in Rate
CAD-USD	Jan. 1	0.860720	N/A
CAD-USD	Jan. 2	0.852122	-0.008598
CAD-USD	Jan. 3	0.848572	-0.003550

Exchange Rates

Fund ID	Balance/Trans -action Type	Bal. Date	Cur- rency	Amount
3	Opening Bal	Jan. 1	CAD	737.32
3	Fees Paid	Jan 3	CAD	(3.45)

Source System Transactions

Fd. ID	Balance/Trans- action Type	Bal. Date	Cur- rency	Amount
3	Bal. Conversion	Jan. 1	USD	634.63
3	Bal. Revaluation	Jan. 2	USD	(6.34)
3	Bal. Revaluation	Jan 3	USD	(2.62)
3	Fee Paid Conv.	Jan 3	USD	(2.93)

Currency Exchange Transactions

A Canadian fund requires conversion into US dollars, each transaction converted at the day's rate, each new day's balance revalued for any change in exchange rate; all these transactions, summarized as balances, and then used in US dollar reports. (See Appendix for calculations)

Table 13 – Foreign Currency Example

4. Perform other analytical processes, such as multi-currency, and apply those transactions to the balances as well.

All these steps would typically be done throughout the night, immediately following the source data system daily processing.*

In summary, the breadth of the outputs possible from our data supply chain is dependent upon the level of detail in this part of the assembly line. If we assemble all of the "laptop" except the display, then we can vary only that one component on the output. If we discard most of the transaction-level attributes of potential interest early in the supply chain, our potential outputs will similarly be limited.

On the other hand, if we can vary 20 components in our manufacturing processes, we can produce unlimited much broader number of different outputs. If we have these customer contract attributes available in the next stage of manufacturing, we can produce a huge number of outputs.

All the web crawling and database populating performed continually prior to a web search are hidden from the person entering a query—but it is critical to satisfying the query in a reasonable time. All preparatory work on the quantitative analytical side is similarly invisible to the end user. But it is critical to the next step: producing the final outputs.

---

* We've assumed throughout this book that radical changes to the source data systems are out of bounds. If we were able to make operational data structures consistently across all source data systems, we may ask the source data systems to prepare and hold the raw materials necessary for manufacturing answers. Requiring this elongates the implementation timeframe dramatically.

Additionally, we've assumed given the age of most of these source data systems in most large organizations, they are typically batch processes. The principles are the same, however, for real-time systems. If the buckets maintained for analysis remain daily (rather than hourly or something shorter), real time system data will accumulate in the posting engine until the period end for final posting.

Fund ID	Fund Name	Risk Type	Date Purchased
1	Fund A	Aggressive	1998
2	Fund B	Aggressive	2001
3	Fund C	Moderate	1998
4	Fund D	Conservative	1998
5	Fund E	Aggressive	2000

Mutual Fund Attribute Tables

Fund ID	Balance/Trans -action Type	Balance Date	Amount
1	Opening Bal	January 1	1,020.00
1	Dividends	January 3	10.00
1	Fees Paid	January 5	-7.56
2	Opening Bal.	January 1	378.00
3	Opening Bal	January 1	737.32
3	Fees Paid	January 3	-3.45
4	Opening Bal	January 1	247.31
4	Shr. Purchase	January 4	341.32
5	Opening Bal	January 1	2,320.21
5	Share Sold	January 3	-310.21

Low-level Balance or Transaction Table

Table 14 – Multiple Report Input Example

Mutual Funds by Risk Type		
Risk Type: Aggressive		
Fund A	1,022.44	
Fund B	378.00	
Fund E	2,010.00	
Total Risk Type, Aggressive		3,410.44

Report 1: Mutual Funds by Risk Type

Mutual Funds by Year Purchased		
Purchase Year: 1998		
Fund A	1,022.44	
Fund C	733.87	
Fund D	588.63	
Total Purchase Year, 1998		2,344.94

Report 2: Mutual Funds by Year Purchased

We can produce both reports above using the prior table input data, by joining Fund IDs, and aggregating by Name, Risk or Date. For example, Fund A, (ID 1) is Aggressive, purchased in 1998. The opening balance of 1,020.00 and an accumulated dividend of 10.00 less fees of 7.56 equal the 1,022.44 above. Opening balances eliminate the need for historical transactions of less value.

Table 15 – Multiple Report Output Example

Chapter 13

HIGH-LEVEL AGGREGATION

Data Supply Chain Part 3

Now we return to the processes that are analogous to an Internet search engine. These remaining steps are where search engines have advanced far beyond the metric engines of yesterday.

Answering an Internet query involves two basic steps: Select and sort. A metric query will require these two steps, and one more: summarize or aggregate. We have performed one level of aggregation in the low-level posting, but most analytical queries require much more aggregation.

We are all quite familiar with the selection process in an Internet query. The function would need to be close to the same in our metric engine, but there are a few differences worth noting.

First, be clear that our metric engine needs to be selecting low-level balances records linked to customer or vendor and contract details *to be used* in the final set aggregation process. In other words, we must select before we aggregate. This is necessary to answer questions like "What is the total ticket value of all elite frequent flyers who flew to Florida last week?" We have to select Florida flights by frequent flyers before we can aggregate to the total value metric.

Second, with the data we're likely to get today, we have a bit of a syntax problem. Structured data for the most part, doesn't have the descriptors on it that text on web pages have. So the data might contain the value "31" in the "company number" position, not some readable text like "Company 31". This obviously can be overcome in some way, either through the translation process (which might increase data volumes if the newly assigned tags have to be stored) or through the query process (which might increase the response time for the user building a query).

In both an Internet and a metric search we vary the length of the query—and thus the specificity of the query—depending on our needs. In some cases we want a range of records, for example, the total sales for each product sold in New York and Ohio. The query would find all sales transactions in the states of New York and Ohio, but to aggregate correctly, the transaction must also contain the product number. We don't want the total for *all* products in a state; we want the total for *each* product in *each* state.

To do this, the computer will need to be able to accumulate all transactions for each state and product. So after selecting the transactions to accumulate for the balance or balances, the next step is to sort these records. In this example, we would sort the transactions in order by state and by product during the aggregation of these records. When the computer encounters a new state or product, it begins a new accumulator.

Internet search engines perform a form of sorting when attempting to rank the pages most likely to be of interest at the top of the results. Our metric processing requires sorting to facilitate aggregation.

We must allow for a difference between the order in which the fields appear on the transaction record or stored in our system and the order in which they are sorted. Predefining which accumulators will be held is a form of a static posting process.

Another optional step at this point is performing calculations in some way to manipulate the balance. In certain instances, the low-level posted balance is adjusted based upon dates, risks, and other types of factors. This process is creating a new balance, perhaps temporary (and perhaps un-posted) to be summarized in the last step.

The last step for many types of analysis is to summarize or aggregate the transactions. The contrast from a textual search is important. A textual search can present a new page of results each time a user clicks Next; if the internet engine's index presents data in relevance order, each click requires only one more page of data to be read and displayed.

Aggregation is different. Aggregation requires that the engine must use each record to accumulate the overall aggregated balance. Thus, the data volumes for this step of the process become much higher than those for a typical textual search, which has a natural pause between each click of the Next button.

Let's also add that in our query we need to be able to specify at what "level" we want to produce subtotals or balances. Do we want balances for all of New York, or for each Store in New York, or for each Customer at each Store in New York, or for each Product purchased by each Customer in each Store in New York? This discussion could continue by considering hierarchies, roll-ups, reorganizations, recursion, and more, but in the interest of brevity, we'll forbear.

OK, so now we've completed our comparison between the Internet search engine and the metric engine I'm proposing. But we haven't examined the most important point. Consider how quickly an Internet search engine trolls through the myriad individual web pages to give us an answer to our question.

Instead of creating answers to predefined questions, it allows us to ask any question we want. This is just-in-time manufacturing at its best—nearly instantaneous manufacturing to our textual questions.

We could never hope to accomplish the same thing if we tried to use individual transactions with today's technology. But creating intermediate balances at a low level of detail may make it possible to do so, or at least get closer. Given enough compute capacity, users may query lower and lower levels of detail to achieve the transparency needed. Effectively drilling down is simply creating another query in an automated way. Such a system would be very powerful indeed.

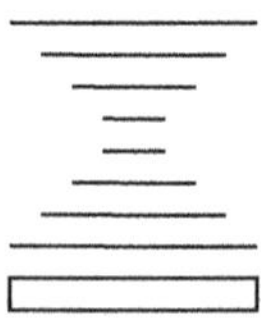

From a distance, the system might look a little bit like two pyramids stacked on top of each other. From the tremendous diversity in the source data system layer, with tens of thousands of attributes, business events would be organized into a few attributes classifying detailed balances in the middle, and then pivoted into tens of thousands of analytical outputs at the request of the end users at the other end of the system.

Chapter 14

SCALE

Producing the Goods

Steps 1 and 2 of our manufacturing process typically happen the same way throughout each night. Yet if we wish to avoid the traps of predefined posting processes, step 3, high-level aggregation, must be allowed to vary each day and need to happen much closer to the time of query. Doing so requires very efficient use of our computing resources.

We must combine the low-level posted balances and then join them with static data about customers, vendors, and products accessing additional attributes in very specific ways very quickly. The more difficult questions to answer are not about one specific customer's mortgage balance; we can use the source data system for that. A more difficult problem is calculating the average mortgage balance for all loans maturing in the next six months. This requires accumulations of data from many sources or from long periods or both. This might also require processing large numbers of low-level balances.

As we've noted, the critical issue is the speed of computers. The convoluted nature of today's data supply chains is primarily a reaction to the speed of processing.

To provide answers to questions with a reasonable response time, our legacy systems post to summary structures, reducing the response time for the query because each answer is readily available in the posted file. This reduction in user response

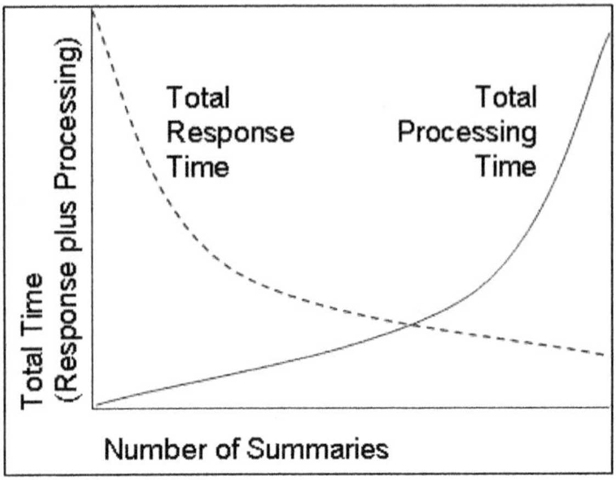

Figure 4 - Summary Response Impact

time continues as more and more summaries are created, to answer more and more questions.

However, correspondingly, the system has to perform a posting process for each transaction received against each of these summary structures. This is typically done during the nightly transaction processing cycle, not at report time. At some point, the reduction in response time for a user is less than the additional update time for posting because not all answers in the summaries are used.

This interior minimum point is likely reached in most organizations with today's system configuration, at the expense of being able to easily answer questions not provided by the existing supply chains, and the cost of supply chains that are no longer insightful.

This point is typically met within a geography by the start of the query process, which typically is the start of the business day. In most environments the major data supply chains cannot begin until after the source data system end-of-day processes are complete. This is in the early hours of the morning for those with the highest volumes or most complexity.*

And because there are a set of balances that must be created to manage the business first thing in the day (Graphs 3, 4 and 5), this becomes the critical point at which the data supply chain must produce the majority of balances required, to minimize reconciliation between different data supply chains.

This leaves a space of perhaps four or five hours for the data supply chains to process data gathering (step 1 in Chapter 11) and low-level posting (step 2 in Chapter 12).

Historically, by using summarization either in the source data systems or soon after, these existing systems typically operate on tens of thousands to hundreds of thousands of records.† Time typically needs to be reserved to handle unexpected conditions, and so typical processing is tuned to finish in perhaps two hours' time.

Targeting our low-level posting process to keep customer contract details has an explosive effect on the volumes processed in the major data supply chains. In banking, for example, a sizable organization might have 20 million customers, each customer holding perhaps two or more accounts, like checking and a car loan, for example. This means the low-level balances maintained in the system are

---

* A global organization is typically partitioned by major geographic locations, providing perhaps three major regions for end-of-day processing: EMEA, Americas, and Asia.

Rewriting all the source data systems, valued in millions and in some cases tens of millions of dollars in investment, is consider impractical for making real progress on these issues in a timely manner.

† This is typically the General Ledger level volumes.

typically multiplied by 40 million or more when compared to summary level supply chains like the General Ledger.

Organizations do not keep a lot of spare compute capacity on the shop floor due to costs. It's absurd to think that the technology used to process tens and hundreds of thousands of records can be scaled without enormous expenditure (if it's even possible) to tens of millions of balances with the associated posting processes.

How then should we configure them to solve the basic posting problem more effectively? Remember that computers are like a meeting, with people for CPUs, a whiteboard for fast temporary memory, and a binder for slow permanent memory. (See chapter 8)

To speed things up, many reporting applications now store large amounts of data in an in-memory database, satisfying a very large number of reports that only a few years ago would be unthinkable. But we shouldn't assume that all data for all permutations of reports at the transaction level will cheaply fit into memory.

If we design as if everything will fit into memory, we may have a critical constraint if it does not; this memory limitation may become the output constraint for the data supply chain. Assuming at least some disk configuration will reduce the cost and provide a safety net should we need one.

Let's be clear about the challenges of using large amounts of disk. Disk is so much slower than memory, 1,000 times slower than memory. No one will use the metric engine if, upon clicking "search," instead of waiting 1 second we wait 1000 seconds—over 15 minutes!

So how do we make access to the data in the binder faster? Well, one way is to create indexes, which means we would bring smaller amounts of data into memory to search for the location of the exact data we want. This is one approach to the problem.

However, indexes for data tend to be like indexes in books, where someone has to decide what will be important to search for so the index can be created. Also, the index doesn't often give us the data we need; just like a book index, we have to turn from it to the actual page to find the data. So, in some cases indexes simply end up using more memory, disk and processing time.

If we have enough outputs to produce from the same data, it can be more efficient to organize it for a massive scan, wherein we go through the database once. Perhaps this is the lowest cost alternative, sacrificing a bit of production immediacy for periodic production of many more outputs.

Doing so requires that we organize the data to be scanned for the massive, one-time process. When we have a huge number of reports to produce, we can load all data for a particular customer contract or vendor contract into memory at one time. This isn't all data for all contracts; we only load that data related to a single customer contract into memory at one time. Then all reports have access to it for use in all reports to be produced in that scan of the data. After they have used that data, the next contract is brought into memory.

This is a bit of the best of both worlds: In-memory use for a subset of data, allowing for efficient load of the memory from disk at the same time.

As an example, all types of information needed for the reports—all the information about each of our funds, all the fund attributes like risk and fund manager, all the purchase transactions, all the sales transactions, even daily point-in-time balances for some portion of history—are brought into memory at one time. Because the various record types for a single contract all exist in memory all at once, they can be joined together very efficiently; all the attributes on all records are available for selection, sort, or aggregation. This technique creates a very data-rich environment for a very short period.

Greater usefulness comes if the additional low-level processes like multi-currency can be performed during this same scan of the data; the needed transactions are generated and applied all within this same process. The usefulness of our data is limited without these processes, and reading and writing all the data to perform these functions would consume a large portion of this precious window for processing.

The reports that are the more difficult ones to produce aggregate large amounts of data, but the end output tends to be very small; often they fit into a spreadsheet. It is possible to allocate a portion of memory to each of the reports being produced from this scan, and begin initial sort and aggregation processes immediately upon record selection. This allows us to manage the very high data volumes required for the aggregation phase. This approach uses all the compute resources very effectively.

Some have likened this to the effectiveness of mass transit as opposed to individual cars: All travelers needing to get somewhere use the same vehicle, and all reports requiring low-level data share the same access to it. Mass transit requires a synchronized start for all travelers, and all queries must also start at the same time, a slight disadvantage to this approach.

However, taking this approach has some interesting side benefits. This same tooling may be useful in the low-level posting process of preparing the inputs for manufacturing, for aren't those steps the same as a balance assembly line? The only difference is that one set of outputs is stored as the input for the next time.

No matter which approach we take, a method of performing parallel processing must be used in both options. Parallel processing is a way of accomplishing more work in the same amount of time by using more than one CPU to do the work, like having more people in our conference room analogy, and even more conference rooms for more people.

Aggregation will require, in the end, all the data selected to be brought together onto whiteboards in one room for merging, if not sorting and summarizing.

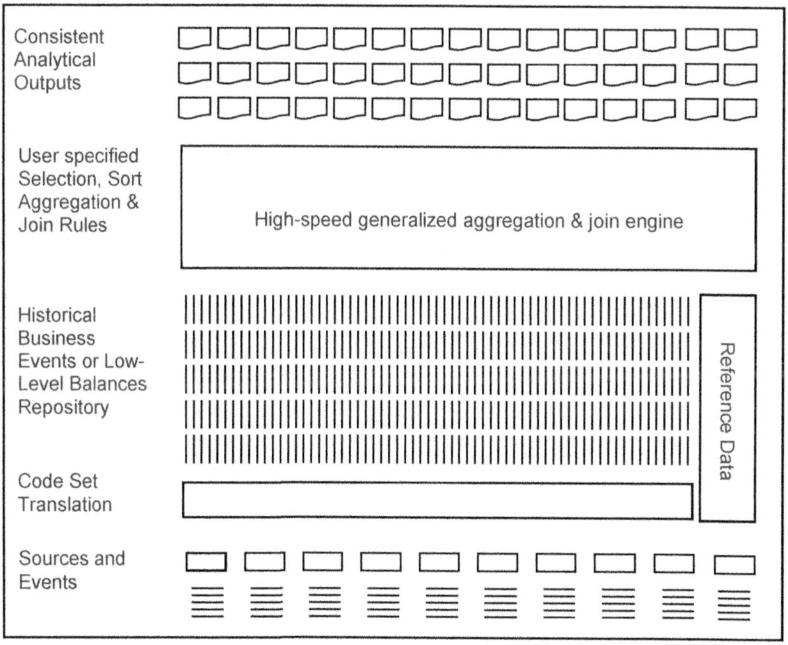

Figure 5 – Quantitative Aggregation Engine

The speed and scale of this final aggregation process determines the breadth of the potential outputs for our assembly line.

The concepts just discussed are very different than all but a couple of posting processes I am familiar with, but they have been proven to work. These aren't small little theoretical test cases either; these are mission critical book of record financial systems processes for a Fortune 500 financial services firm and for one of the world's largest banks, each operating now for years. For example, on a daily basis these systems do this type of work:

- In 30 minutes of elapsed time and about 3 hours of parallel processing time, 2.4 billion records are read, extracting summarized and detail records totaling 72 million records, doing nearly 1 billion joins producing hundreds of outputs.
- Starting at 3 AM, 19 million transactions are exploded into 200 million entries, which are posted against a 7 billion row master file, which is also revalued for multi-currency and other financial functions, and all this completes by 7 AM, producing hundreds of outputs at the same time.

These are real world metric engines.

Chapter 15

DATA REACTIVE FUNCTIONS

Major Data Supply Chains

Let's go back to where we began: metrics for measurement. There are a set of major "data reactive" functions in most organizations today that produce metrics of tremendous value. They can be called data reactive because almost no one enters any new data into them directly and they capture and record almost no new transactions or "business events." Rather, these systems receive, and *react to* the data created earlier in a host of operational systems. The outputs are a myriad of metrics used to measure activities within an organization.

These systems include the financial, risk, and management information systems (MIS) data supply chains.

The oldest of these systems and the historical center of high quality quantitative data—in high-level summary—is the general ledger or GL. It has been developed over decades, with processes honed through incremental improvements and rigorous quality audits enforcing financial reporting standards. It gathers all financial data—highly quantitative—systematically from almost all source data systems which contain financial data today.

The metrics it produces include Net Income, Earnings Before Interest and Taxes (EBIT) Total Revenue and Total Expenses, Total Assets, Total Liabilities, Owner's Equity, and others.

Because of its age, the data in the general ledger is very well known. Although its data is highly anticipated, it is not at the center of most of the recent questions, often because we've used the data to produce all the interesting facts it contains in its summarized format. The advent of the other data supply chains was, in many respects, a reaction to its highly summarized nature.

Building our metric engine begins with gathering high quality data. It does not begin from scratch, but rather with today's trusted system of record, the GL, the system with the quality seal of approval. If our quantitative results match the GL, we will have greater confidence the answer is correct.

The GL summarizes business events by attributes called the accounting code block, or *Chart of Accounts* (COA). Because the GL summarizes data from all source data systems according to this set of fields, the COA becomes a common language running throughout the organization, at least for financial transactions. It provides an organizing principle around which we can build.

My father explained to me once that in order to start a bridge across a canyon, workers would first tie a string to an arrow, and shoot the arrow across to workers on the other side. The workers would then tie the string to a rope, and the workers on the far side would pull across the rope. A cable would then be tied to the rope and pulled across, and another cable would then be pulled back the other way, leading to a temporary bridge enabling the building of the permanent structure. It all began with an arrow and a string.

The GL's COA is the string to allow us to find the high quality data in the source data systems. Its consistency throughout the organization, and the data needed to support it, allows us to understand the data we already have captured. The existing balances in the GL are the arrows. We can prove to ourselves we have captured the high quality data for our analytical engine by tracing these feeds backwards from the GL to the details they originally consumed. These details provide the starting point of the detailed repository.

The finance system, though, tends to be a backwards-facing system. It tells us only what has happened.

The risk systems, specifically those for credit, market, and liquidity risks, tend to be very sophisticated forecasting engines, analyzing many potential outcomes. The risk systems are not as old as the finance system, but are becoming increasingly critical, particularly in financial services. In insurance companies, they predict what potential losses might be; in banking, they explain the cumulative standing of customers and trading partners. Regulations are developing rapidly to make them as rigorous as the finance system.

Today, the risk and finance systems are fed as two distinct supply chains. When the finance system's historical perspective catches up to the risk projections, differences between expected and actual results may be due to two variables: inaccurate risk models *and* inconsistent data in the supply chains. Consolidating data supply chains by increasing the detail of finance data provides a feed to the risk systems and eliminate one variable, increasing assessed risk accuracy.

The result? Higher quality risk models from feedback from high quality historical data, resulting in higher quality quantitative analytics.

Are there other business events—perhaps non-financial or at least non-GL transactions—required to answer the risk system needs? Of course there are. Our metric engine will need to include these new business events, but the principles of

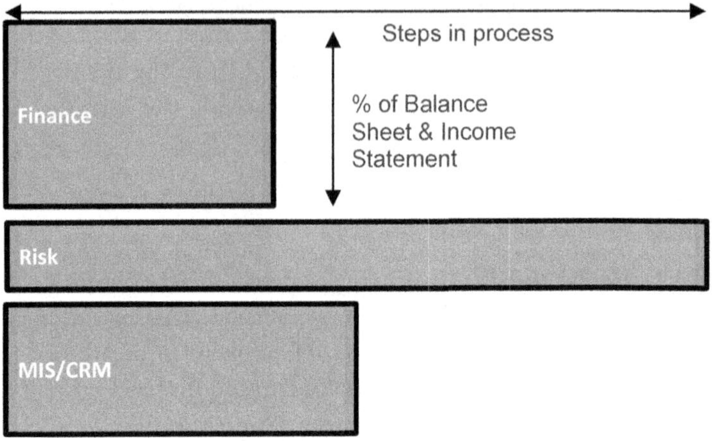

Figure 6 –Data Function Widths and Lengths

processing these are likely very similar at least in the initial steps.

The depth and width of these data reactive functions vary. The width of the function in Figure 6 represents the types of metrics that must be kept, and the length of the function represents the number of steps in the data supply chain. For example, the finance data supply chain is quite wide (it must keep track of all the balances for the balance sheet and income statement for the enterprise), but the number of steps are relatively short, including accounting rules application, adjustment, multi-currency, etc.

The risk system is more narrow in its concerns. For example, it does not care about buildings or supplies expenses. But the number of steps required in the risk data supply chain is much longer. Simply accumulating customer and counterparty balances is only the beginning. Other processes follow: stress testing, scenario generation, and the calculation of various metrics, such as loss given default and probability of default.

For example, a customer's outstanding loan to the bank may be multiplied by a measure of that person's estimated potential inability to pay: 0% for low risk customers and 100% for those who are unlikely to pay the loan back. A metric engine can accumulate these transactions to estimate projected losses.

In some instances, there are interdependencies between these functions even in today's independent data supply chains. For example, the risk system will calculate a loan loss reserve, which is included in the finance system. Our new system would also need to allow the addition of new metrics based upon the results of analysis of existing quantitative data.

The last major data reactive function is the Management Information System (MIS), sometimes called performance management system or key performance indicator (KPI) system. This system was developed to measure internal company performance, and has historically been closely linked to the financial system, because the financial system provided many of the needed metrics, but not all.

Whereas the GL measured overall company performance, or perhaps divisions and departments, MIS evaluated employee and management performance. What are the sales per sales person? What is the profit for a particular store? How much did support functions like finance and risk cost?

Perhaps the ledger provided these answers, but if not, MIS added other attributes not captured in the GL. If there was a type of report that required a different view of the data than accounting standards required, it was done in the MIS system. If additional non-financial attributes were needed, MIS could capture the transactions.

The MIS system didn't have the same data quality standards as the financial system; it just had to be good enough that employees and management couldn't argue with the results.

And the challenges in this system have been quite clear; more metrics would allow measurement of more things, with potential improvements in more areas. Yet the ability of the systems to gather data for new measurement has been severely limited. Continuing regulatory changes in the finance and risk systems have consumed discretionary spending which could have been applied to MIS. In addition, the nature of the systems precludes flexibility; posting processes provide predetermined answers.

One of the major areas of potential innovation in the MIS space is getting to true customer profitability and service costing models. This is where the real innovation lies, because it unleashes the creativity of the people in the organization. Rather than complying with regulations, they can come to understand customers, products, services, costs, and processes, all through measurement.

All three of these data supply chains measure things. What they measure differs, but a great deal of the input data used for measurement is shared. If we overlaid the bars in Table 6, the overlapped area is very valuable, common data.

Greater flexibility in our measurement systems may have dramatic, and in fact unexpected consequences.

Chapter 16

CONSOLIDATION

The Impact of Change

Looking back, we can see that it was difficult to predict every way the Internet changed our lives, personally and professionally. No one seems to have been completely right. Perhaps some predictions were overstated, but no one can say that the impact has been small and unnoticed. Search engines have proven tremendously valuable in increasing productivity. The value of innovation in this space has paid for itself many times over.

It is similarly difficult to guess at what the benefits might be for a more streamlined quantitative analytical engine. The changes may be just as profound, though. It is likely that investments in a new breed of metric engine will eliminate the need to maintain multiple systems, all of which accumulate quantitative data.

Incremental improvements in metrics engines have been made and continue to be made largely in the data reactive systems such as finance, risk and MIS described above, especially in the financial services sector. Drivers specifically for this industry for metric engines include:

- Cost Reductions from (1) reduced development time for creation of new reports and analysis (2) less reconciliation, and (3) lower cost for compliance reporting.

- Increased Productivity from (1) availability of data with common codes, definitions, granularity and frequency, and (2) the flexibility to change the functional operating model.
- Improved Allocation of Capital, Liquidity Management, and Performance Metrics through (1) improved understanding of risk and capital usage from portfolio to product levels, (2) quicker management actions to avoid losses via quicker trend reads from reliable Risk and Finance figures, (3) improved new-customer targeting and credit extension and (4) improved customer netting.
- Improved Regulatory/Stake Holder confidence through (1) reduction in regulatory capital requirements, and (2) credibility with regulators from cleaner source data, fewer reconciliations and breaks, cross-validated risk / financial results, and more frequent analytics.

These predictions are not theoretical; very large organizations have proven the fundamental principles actually work, and the trajectory for innovation is correct.

Let's go back to some of those simple examples in chapter 1 and imagine what the process might look like in the future:

Revenues An executive responsible to approve pricing on a major deal for a global client uses a simple query to accumulate the top 100 customers by using the global customer identifier of revenue by year for the last three years. This request uses the low-level postings, and accumulates the daily balances to arrive at each year's values. Joins are used to get to the customer, accumulating customers with more than one product or contract.* A pass through all customers is required, evaluating each to see if it qualifies as a top 100.

With this simple query in hand, suppose the executive notices this customer is not in the top 50 customers, perhaps casting doubt upon the proposed offered price.

Because of the highly aggregated nature of today's financial systems, fulfilling this simple request is often not possible. Only with an improved, more detailed data supply chain, could it be done.

Risk and Forecasting Imagine that upon reflection the executive realizes a major product shift could be skewing the historical trends. So the executive decides to add another column to the report containing a simple risk adjusted forecast of those revenues. To do this, perhaps the executive selects only revenue based upon the new product line, excluding the historically larger but declining product, and uses a weighted average of buying trends over time. The executive multiplies this by the internal risk department's local customer (not the global customer ID) risk rating, which is based upon detailed divisional financial measures and more accurate than the global company ratings.

This new metric gives a sense of the trend of the customer relative to the more important new product, and their ability to fulfill the contract requirements. This requires selecting and pivoting our low-level balances by product type, and including new, non-finance measures of risk assessment by customer. This report might show that this customer is number one in the world for the new product line and financial ability to pay.

---

* A recursive call up a customer hierarchy may be necessary to arrive at the global customer identifier.

Today's risk and forecast systems are typically almost completely separate from the financial systems, so combining them into a single analysis at any level but the highest company or geographic level is impossible. Only by consolidating these data supply chains would this analysis be possible.

Profit. Having examined revenue and risk, our executive is ready to think about profit. Suppose the executive adds another column to the report. Remember, costs don't typically accumulate because we paid something to a customer; rather they accumulate from payments to vendors, employees, suppliers, even overhead departments like real estate and so on. But these costs can be organized in the same way as our customer/contract metrics, with base metrics and joins to vendor and other attributes.

Yet we still have a problem: Our report is sorted and aggregated by customers, and our cost data cannot be. So, this process will not be one which simply accumulates data from the source data systems; rather, an intermediate analytical process will be required to get to a unit cost. Our executive might use data someone else has generated to calculate unit costs.

But what if the executive wanted to calculate his own unit costs? One simple measure would be to take the total costs for the company for some period of time, divided by the number of units or all products produced or sold during the same period. So our new system has to have the ability to store new data which can be used as input to another query.*

* An interesting element of banking is that the financial balances as represented in deposits are the majority of the raw material for the loans. So funds transfer pricing is a type of allocation or internal pricing to determine the cost and value of funds.

Perhaps such analysis shows our executive that the proposed pricing for the contract will result in a loss on the contract.

This sort of analysis could produce tremendous new insights about how costs flow through the organization. Such flexibility is impossible for all but the smallest organizations and data. Yet such analysis would almost certainly improve most organizational results.

Unit Costs The decision on the contract really depends upon these costs. Suppose the executive senses a need to drill down on the costs involved. Doing so is the process of executing more and more specific queries targeting the data selected for drill down.

Suppose the executive finds that a major component of the new product unit costs is an allocated cost for a department that has historically been allocated to all products, but provides limited support for the new product. If this cost is eliminated, the contract price provides an adequate profit per unit.

Here's a case where transparency highlights an outmoded analytical approach; the allocated department is a cost that will diminish as the old product line declines.

This type of measurement is critical to improving our products and services. This type of insight is essential to moving to the next level in our economic activities. Better quantification of the increasing amounts of data can force us to understand our complex world more thoroughly, and encourage us to take more effective actions.

EPILOGUE

Study history I was once told. I've attempted to outline where quantification might go next, the foundations of a metric engine, its purpose, how it would need to operate, and the resulting types of functions it might enable. One question not answered is how it might be funded.

In my years of experience in this space, I have worked in various industries. I have gravitated toward financial services because metric engine functions are closely related to the core of those businesses. Thus, most of the examples in this book come from this space. Yet all organizations have finance departments. They all deal with quantitative analysis.

The data reactive function drivers will continue to motivate incremental improvements in finance, risk and MIS functions if for no other reason than public policy as expressed in regulations will require greater accuracy and transparency in decisions making.

Yet because these data reactive functions are still primarily support functions to the core business, even in financial services, this work is not likely to cause a major acceleration in the development of a metric engine.

A more transformative capability, building upon these data reactive functions, would be risk adjusted customer profitability. It combines the results from finance, risk and

MIS into a single analytical output. Because of its focus on customers specifically, this function has significant potential to affect how an organization behaves, financial services or other industries; parts of the organization are no longer motivated to exploit gaps between the data reactive analytical functions.

Risk adjusted customer profitability, though, can still be built in a manner removed from the core functions of the business. Those core functions are usually isolated in the product systems. In financial services, these core systems support the creation and sales of financial products like loans, deposits, etc., pricing those products using interest rates and fees, and managing customer accounts and functions.

Almost all of the analytics of these core processes are at the heart of metric engine outputs. Development of products, assessment of individual risks, customized pricing… all these things would be radically altered through a more flexible metric engine. I believe a major metric engine business would likely use a financial services business model in some way. The financial services functions are at the heart of a metric engine.

So financial services will be significantly impacted if and when a true metric engine of the simplicity and scale of search engines is developed. Yet just like the information providers of the late 90's did not create the great Internet search engines, financial services firms may not be the first to create a true metric engine. The weight of the fragmented legacy system environments may significantly inhibit them.

Who else might accelerate the development of a true metric engine? Perhaps a search engine? As we have compared here, they have many of the functions in place to do so. It is very possible they may take on this new, expanded problem.

However, the business model for these businesses today is quite different. The search engines business is based upon advertising. The cost of the "materials" they sell—the search results—are effectively free to search engines; people publish them on websites. Quantitative data will not be so easily procured. Quantitative data, like a customer transaction, is typically highly valued, and not released to everyone. The language of the data today is not the same as spoken language, which the search engines use today, further complicating the efforts.

The value derived from a metric engine may justify a subscription model, but probably cannot be provided at advertising rates. Therefore, although it is certainly possible search engines may take this on, it is not certain they will.

Might someone else develop a metric engine? Another possible industry is telecommunications. Telecoms have been managing large amounts of data for years because most consumers interact with no other business as frequently as they do with telecommunications providers. Call detail, recording who talked to whom, for how long, where and when is very voluminous. Telecom providers know how to manage large amounts of data.

However, although today's telecom data is being used for more and more sophisticated purposes like these discussed in metric engines, historically call detail is not typically manipulated and added up in all the different ways financial data is. Posting processes create balances for minutes used or remaining, but time is typically not as broad a measure as value measured in monetary terms. Even so, it is possible they could add these capabilities.

My guess is that if a significant acceleration in the development of metric engines is to occur, it will likely be in one of these three industries, and it will likely rely upon the revenue models of financial services. However, Internet search engines did not necessarily come out of an existing industry. And all industries have some level of quantitative metric analysis, in at least the finance area. So, the development could come from a very different direction.

Whether the development of a true metric engine accelerates or simply continues more slowly as it has for the last couple of decades, someday more powerful metric engines like the one I have described will come along. The trajectory is quite clear, tracked now over centuries.

Study history? Consider the analysis of the causes of western advances during the Middle Ages by noted history professor Alfred W. Crosby. He argues the West developed a new way of thinking called "Businesslike."

> Businesslike means careful and meticulous and, in practice, is a matter of numbers. It was one of the trails that led to science and technology insofar as its practitioners were quantitative in their perception and manipulation of as much of experience as could be described in terms of quanta. In their case the quanta were money - florins, ducats, livres, pounds, and so on....
>
> Double-entry bookkeeping was and is a means of soaking up and holding in suspension and then arranging and making sense out of masses of data that previously had been spilled and lost....Today computers compute faster than friar Pacioli would ever have dreamed possible, but they do so within the same framework (accounts payable, accounts receivable, and all) as he did. The efficient friar taught us how to oblige grocery stores and nations, which are always whizzing about like hyperactive children, to stand still and be measured....

In the past seven centuries bookkeeping has done more to shape the perceptions of more bright minds than any single innovation in philosophy or science. While a few people pondered the words of Rene Descartes and Immanuel Kant, millions of others of yeasty and industrious inclination wrote entries in neat books and then rationalized the world to fit their books…

In practical terms, the new approach was simply this: reduce what you are thinking about to the minimum required by its definition; visualize it on paper, or at least in your mind, be it the fluctuation of wool prices at the Champagne fairs or the course of Mars through the heavens, and divide it, either in fact or imagination, into equal quanta. Then you can measure it, that is, count the quanta.

Then you possess a quantitative representation of your subject that is, however simplified, even in its errors and omissions, precise. You can think about it rigorously. You can manipulate it and experiment with it, as we do today with computer models. It possesses a sort of independence from you. It can do for you what verbal representation rarely does; contradict your fondest wishes and elbow you on to more efficacious speculation. It was quantification, not aesthetics, not logic per se, that parried Kepler's every effort to thrust the solar system into a cage of his beloved Platonic solids and goaded him on until he grudgingly devised his planetary laws.*

---

* Alfred W. Crosby, The Measure Of Reality: Quantification And Western Society, 1250-1600 (Cambridge University Press, 1997) Pages 200, 220, 221, 228.

APPENDIX: CURRENCY EXCHANGE CALCULATIONS

The tables on the following page describe the calculations used to produce Foreign Currency Example Table 13 on page 75.

Quantitative metric analysis requires establishing consistency in units before performing certain mathematical functions, like aggregation. This is the purpose of foreign exchange calculations.

In a simple way, a transaction must be converted to the foreign currency at the rate applicable when the transaction took place. For example if the transaction takes place at 1:00 PM, then the rate in effect then should be used.

After that time, the balance in the foreign currency must be revalued to reflect changes in the exchange rate. This could be done by again simply multiplying the outstanding balance with the new rate as of that point in time. This approach, though, will leave unanswered the question what was the effect of changes in exchange rates? One could subtract the two balances to get to effect. A more common approach is to multiple the last revalued balance by the *change* in exchange rate since then, storing this transaction, which when accumulated with other transactions answers the effect question.

There are many more aspects to just this specific problem, and many other similar types of processes, like elimination processes, which take out transactions within a unit so they don't gross up the activity. Yet all of these processes can create transactions, which can be used just like any other transaction. Creating and posting these transactions is the most complex part of the work the metric engine will have to do.

Given this input data:

Currency	Date	Rate	Change in Rate
CAD-USD	Jan. 1	0.860720	N/A
CAD-USD	Jan. 2	0.852122	-0.008598
CAD-USD	Jan. 3	0.848572	-0.003550

Fund ID	Balance/Transaction Type	Bal. Date	Currency	Amount
3	Opening Bal	Jan. 1	CAD	737.32
3	Fees Paid	Jan 3	CAD	(3.45)

Results in these additional transactions, which must be turned into balances to be used in metric engine analyses:

Fd. ID	Balance/Transaction Type	Bal. Date	Currency	Amount
3	Open Bal. Conv.	Jan. 1	USD	634.63
3	Bal. Revaluation	Jan. 2	USD	(6.34)
3	Bal. Revaluation	Jan 3	USD	(2.62)
3	Fee Paid Conv.	Jan 3	USD	(2.93)

The calculations are as follows

Date	Type	CAD Balance	Exchange Rate or Change	USD Balance
1-Jan	Transaction	737.32	0.860720	634.63
2-Jan	Rate Chg. Effect	737.32	-0.008598	(6.34)
2-Jan	Closing Balance	737.32		628.29
	Proof (bal. x rate)	737.32	0.852122	628.29
3-Jan	Rate Chg. Effect	737.32	-0.003550	(2.62)
3-Jan	Fees Paid	(3.45)	0.848572	(2.93)
3-Jan	Closing Balance	733.87		622.74
	Proof (bal. x rate)	733.87	0.848572	622.74

FIGURES

TABLES

GRAPHS

INDEX

A

B

C

D

N

O

P

Q

R

S

T

Printed in Dunstable, United Kingdom

91222510R00078